Sexperienced

Guide for the Seasoned Woman
Seeking New Possibilities

KATHERINE A. FORSYTHE, MSW

Published by Second Wind Publishing
www.getasecondwind.com
info@getasecondwind.com

ISBN #978-0-9839750-0-7

Editing by Barbara McNichol Editorial

Book design by Mullins Creative

DEDICATION

To Kate and Beth, my beautiful daughters
and my greatest cheerleaders.

TABLE *of* CONTENTS

An Invitation

YOU'RE INVITED TO
PARTAKE IN THE FESTIVITIES

*S*experienced is about getting women talking and laughing and feeling absolutely wonderful about exploring our sexuality. It can happen now that we've lived enough years to know ourselves well. After all, when it comes to intimacy, we're *sexperienced*. We know what we like, and we sure know what we don't like.

This book comes directly out of my **Sex on the Porch** events in which women from ages 50 to 80 talk about what happens between the sheets and in their relationships. Like slumber parties of yore, we cover a limitless range of topics about our feminine sexuality and its accompanying themes. We examine our intimate physical changes. We look at our changing body image. We delve deeply into our relationships with men—how to live with them and know what they are thinking.

Because hitting the refresh button to achieve partner intimacy is critical, we talk about reviving passion in our flat, dull relationships. If we're single, we ponder the joys and challenges of aloneness, and we dive into perils and pleasures of dating.

What's more, we talk about redefining saucy sex and revving up our steamy sides. We share insider knowledge about the best intimacy enhancers, sex books, and DVDs. We even discuss how to renew feelings of intimacy without expecting or demanding traditional sex. At **Sex on the Porch**, we tackle even the toughest issues: surgery and body changes, illness, divorce, marital infidelity, children leaving and coming back home. All of these affect how we express our feminine sexuality.

I'm frequently asked, "Why the name **Sex on the Porch**?" It first came up at a friend's bachelorette party. As we sat on the host's porch, our talk drifted to discussing sex and I naturally evolved as the facilitator. Every woman involved loved the raw honesty that came out of this session. *Sexperienced* continues this tradition.

I also see **Sex on the Porch** as a metaphor for our stage in life, with the porch signifying a relaxed, thoughtful, comfortable time with ourselves. Sitting out on the veranda with friends at twilight connotes permission to discuss "stuff" we might find too uncomfortable to say anywhere else. It's where we can talk about intimate things *without judgment*, where we feel safe and secure.

Highlights from Sex on the Porch

A 67-year-old woman, with the same man for 38 years, is having fantasies about a guy her age at the coffee shop. He sits with her every time she comes in. Is that normal? She's bored with a lifetime of the same sexual routine with her spouse. She's tried everything to spice it up with her partner, but he's not interested. At the same time, she feels more sexually alive than ever. Do other partnered women feel alone, sexually, in their marriage? What about wanting to have an affair? Is that normal?

Another single woman, 59, is without a husband for the first time in 29 years. Do women like her also feel alone sexually? In fact, she feels more sexually alive than ever but can't seem to attract a partner. What's wrong with her that she can't find anyone? Where are the men; they can't *all* be dead! When she's dating online, why doesn't she get a "hit"? Should she lie about her age? Is that normal?

A single woman, 62, with a new partner wants to know if it's okay to want to be spanked and tied up. She's eager to experiment with sex play, but how in the world does she let him know about her desire? Is that normal?

A 57-year-old woman who loves her husband intensely and has always had great sex with him suddenly feels her libido taking a dip—not to mention she's not staying wet "down there." How do other women handle being dry and having sex that hurts? How can she be sensitive to his ego in the face of his erectile dysfunction and her low libido? What are alternatives to intercourse? Do other women have similar concerns? Is that normal?

A 60-year-old single woman waited until the end of a session to get up the nerve to ask about a man she'd dated four times. She told us he had come out of the bedroom in the morning wearing her pink frilly silk robe—a giant erection beneath it. She asked, "Is that normal for him to wear *my* fussy robe after our first night sleeping together?"

Another woman queried about when her new boyfriend can't get an erection. "Is it because I don't keep him turned on?" Someone else asked how to get her boyfriend to wear a condom. "Is this *normal* at our age to wear condoms, or am I being picky when I ask him to put one on?"

A 68-year-old woman asked if her choice to be celibate is normal. Is celibacy okay?

A 73-year-old woman admitted with embarrassment that she wanted him to use a cucumber—a *cucumber*—as a dildo. She desperately wanted to know, "Is that normal? Is it safe? Or is it sick and twisted?"

What's the biggest outcome of **Sex on the Porch**? We discover that our sexuality is still delightful to talk about, laugh about, cry about, complain about, worry about, mourn about, be amazed about—complete with moments of wondering "do people really *do* that and can I do it, too? Is that *normal*?"

At midlife-plus, we experience a tsunami of change as sexual women. How we adapt to change in our sexuality is key. In the '60s and '70s, we fancied ourselves as invulnerable, immortal, and radical. Today, many of those women who revolutionized women's sexuality question themselves as being desirable and attractive. As female sexual beings after menopause, we especially wonder where and how each of us uniquely fits into today's youth-centric culture. And our questions are endless:

- Am I normal?

- Are other women having a burst of sexual desire? Or are their libidos shrinking?

- Does anyone else dread looking in fitting room mirrors?

- Can men my age still be interested in me? What do they think about women *their* age? Exactly what are they looking for?

- Are other women curious about trying new things—from self-pleasuring to celibacy?

- Can anyone understand my sexual fears and worries about being a woman in my 50s, 60s, 70s?

- Is there hope for me?

Enjoying our sexuality—enjoying all of who we are for all of our lives—can be the secret ingredient that keeps us alive, vital, beautiful, and energized. Yes, we can sizzle in bed and on the boulevard, with or without a partner. Pop singer Cyndi Lauper got it right when she sang, "Girls just wanna have fun-un." Yep, that includes girls over 55, 65, 75. We can be like Tina, 61, who looked me right in the eye and demanded, "I want to feel sexy and have fun, again, right now." Start now!

How *Sexperienced* Helps You Celebrate You!

Because a woman's sexuality is meant to be *fun for a lifetime*, I'd like to invite you to partake in the festivities to re-energize, re-vitalize, re-invigorate!

Throughout this book, you'll find golden nuggets of information that are a must-read—non-negotiables. You'll also find Highlights from **Sex on the Porch** depicting real-life situations (possibly like yours?) discussed at the **Sex on the Porch** events. Titillating Tips are just that—read them all. Red Flag! leaves an important warning. Kat's Quips are captured gems from my 23 years of experience in the field of human sexuality.

My mission for you in writing *Sexperienced* mirrors my intentions for the women at **Sex on the Porch**—that is, to answer critical questions about sexuality so you can feel re-energized about being a sensual seasoned woman.

Sexperienced gives you a mix of all of these elements: inspiration, encouragement, support, education, normalizing, and permission to voice feelings and needs as women—with a hefty dose of levity and amusement. You'll see that, just like **Sex on the Porch**, sometimes I have the solution and sometimes *the group* does—like the woman who showed us how to put on a condom with her teeth. *Much better than anything you'd see on Reality TV!*

Realize that this book is not intended as a manual or research document. Rather, it's a guide to living a full life for yourself—and perhaps to entertaining a lover or ten or even *none*—along the journey. Most important, it gives you permission to explore your sexuality and shows you how to do so. I guarantee you'll find the ideas both reassuring and surprising.

PART I: OWN IT! leads to knowing that sexuality is alive, well, and exhilarating in the seasoned woman who brings a rich history of choices to the discussion. Part I examines your choices and invites you to gently put some of your longstanding habits in the Goodwill bag. I'll not only give you permission to let go of old habits, I'll *show you how.*

PART II: AM I NORMAL? answers the question everyone is asking. Learning how "normal" you are will be both revealing and reassuring. After completing the checklists, you might find yourself surprised and delighted by your delicious reactions to notions in the intimacy arena. Here's what you'll learn as you explore:

- where you feel comfortable with intimacy
- what new ideas you can add to your repertoire
- which activities are a pleasant "reach" for you
- what suggestions make you say, "No, that's not my thing to do."

PART III: THE DATING GAME—STARTING OVER lights the fire to get you going in the dating scene, if that's your focus. As you read about the cautionary signs, you'll gain courage to take action.

PART IV: BODY IMAGE—TALES OF AGE GAIN has everything to do with how you see yourself in the mirror so you can feel good about your changing and newly awakened body. It's a big deal, this body image thing amidst this sagless, wrinkle-free youth culture. Sooner or later, the midlife-plus woman encounters age discrimination based on her body image, either real or imagined. Ask any woman past menopause who has to appear naked in front of a new partner. Doubts pop up that never happened at younger ages! How to handle this sags-and-wrinkles reality becomes your challenge. Throughout Part IV, you'll find questions in charts that help you identify where your confidence lies—and where you feel most vulnerable. *(Tip:* Embrace the fact that your seasoned body is as beautiful as you allow it to be.)

Mostly, have a blast with the ideas and encouragement you find in *Sexperienced*. Share your discoveries with your friends. Know that you deserve to have a grand time in the second half of your life.

Celebrate the festivities of being yourself—a sexy seasoned woman.

~ Kat Forsythe, 2011

Part One

OWN IT!

"Why does it take cancer to see how blue the sky is? If I'm not afraid to die, you mustn't be afraid to live! Listen, ladies, you don't have time for negative thinking. Life is meant to be lived! Be sexy. Be zesty. Be luscious. Own it!"
~ Susan Sebastian, 55

At **Sex on the Porch** one evening, women in our group had been groaning and grumbling about getting older, sagging, and losing sex appeal. Then Susan stopped us cold with this bold proclamation of wisdom, quoted above. One year later, she succumbed to cancer. We had no idea that she was on her fifth bout with uterine cancer. To us, she had been a model of life, love, and vitality. We watched Susan die while she taught us how to live. Her remarks that night sounded a wake-up call for all of us.

My wish for you is that you catch the life-giving wave of spirit from Susan. Revive your passion, re-energize your sexuality, re-invigorate your sexy self. Gather inspiration to be a vibrant sensual woman—however you define it—for many years to come. As Susan proclaimed, "Own it!"

Right now, open your mind to the idea that you can rev up your sexy self and your intimate life. Whatever you're facing—life/death, happiness/sadness, vibrant health/challenging illness—you can make *today* a turning point for savoring your sexuality for the rest of your life. We are sexual beings from birth to death and I, for one, plan to celebrate my sexuality to the max—no matter what comes my way. I plan to own it. Want to join me?

Let's begin our quest for optimum sexuality with a snapshot of the landscape we're traversing as women *right now*. What does it look like from the perspective of our sexuality? By the end of Chapter 1, you'll have identified what's going on (or what's not happening), and what you'd like to do about it going forward.

❧

Kat's Quip
Your sexuality. What's sex got to do with it?

Sex is what you do in private. *Sexuality* is who you are in public.

This is an important distinction because it allows for sexual expression in many more places than the bedroom. Think of *sexuality* as an umbrella over all the ways you express your being as a seasoned woman— the way you walk, the words you use, the attitude you present, the clothes you don, the work you do, the wisdom you have about being a woman.

Realistically, the activities you enjoy during a romantic interlude ("having sex") make up only one small piece of the pie. *Sexuality* is much bigger than *sex*—with its many options for expressing it—as you'll soon discover in Chapter 1.

CHAPTER 1

Hey You,
Sexy Seasoned Lady

Look around at your midlife-plus girlfriends. As you observe them, what does "seasoned sexuality" look like, how does it act, what's normal, and how can it get even better? Definitely, your sexuality looks different now than as a 25 year old. That's both the good news and the bad news. Today, you have new challenges, joys, and possibilities.

To determine the current landscape, first of all let's consider our role models. No generation in human history has lived as long as we have. Radically few of us have family role models for seasoned sexiness. Our mothers certainly didn't have the opportunities and life spans that we anticipate enjoying.

What's more, our generation—the leading edge of the Baby Boomers—created the sexual freedom that's taken for granted today. Our openness to new thinking in the late '50s (the beatniks, rock and roll), the '60s (the sexual revolution, Roe vs. Wade, The Pill), and the '70s (communal living, women's rights) set a precedent of expectations that have never deserted us. We found a better, freer way of "being" while expressing our authentic selves.

We Made Up the Rules

When it came to sexuality, we made up new rules. The good news: We're still making them up today, right now, as seasoned women.

The bad news: We're encountering seismic life changes we hadn't accounted for. Better news: As women, we're equipped with the skills to handle the tsunami of change, the sexual freedom, and the opportunity to let our sexuality shine through all of it.

❧

Kat's Quip
But what about …?

What's the impact of serious illness on sexuality, intimacy, and relationships? What about childhood abuse? When either death or divorce looms in our lives, what do they do to us sexually? What about loneliness? What about rape? What about body changes? What about cancer? And what about all of these: Kids leave, lovers move on, partners get old, affairs happen, friends come and go, families transfer, careers change or end, and menopause comes and goes with all of its pendulous mood swings.

The list could go on and on.

At this point, we could identify all the things that hold us back. But we won't. Each of us has our own list, our own issues. Truth told, it's just as Susan Sebastian said, we don't have time for negative energy. And as my friend Kathy Baker told me after her third breast cancer diagnosis: "I cry the first day, drink a lot the second day and call my doc for anti-depressants, eat chocolate the third day, cry again on the fourth day, tell everyone on the fifth day, have a giant pity party on the sixth day, and get spiritually ready for a lot of meditating on the seventh day. Then, I do what the card says: 'Put on my big girl panties and deal with it.'"

Yep, lots of stuff can spoil the fun, no denying it. Many crises can suck the sexuality out of us seasoned women—but only if we let them. I contend that it's all in how we look at it.

My friend Joan Brock, a professional inspirational speaker who is 55+, lost her eyesight to a virus when in her early 30s. Unable to view her daughter's recent wedding, she used all her senses and still "saw" the whole event. Today, Joan is one of the most beautiful, sexy, vivacious women you would ever meet. Her secret? Being thankful every single day for life, for love, for laughter, and for "girl" things like shopping, shoes, make-up, giggling, and all-round looking lovely. Although Joan can't see herself through her eyesight, she is indeed beautiful—and very sexy—inside and out. She sees herself through her soul.

How about you? You're about something brighter than ever, too.

Break the Mold

Sexuality, like life in general, is a work in progress. The way we think of ourselves has changed throughout our lives and will continue to change—without fail. We learn new information. We adapt. We revisit our old messages and update our sexuality—just as we update our financial plans, our diets, our wardrobes, our homes. We scratch out old ways and polish up our lives with new ideas.

That's good! The slate needs to be washed and wiped clean of old messages. Pick up fresh chalk and write anew on that blackboard of life with messages about the updated, present-day *you*. Tell yourself, "That was then, this is now."

Take time to intentionally visit your wants and needs in the areas of intimacy and relationships. Get an untarnished handle on what you're looking for—*now*. Take an updated picture that reflects knowing—with confidence—who you are *right now*, what you want, and with whom (if anyone) you want it.

But how? Chapter 2 gets you started.

Spinning the Wheel
of Your Sexuality

A woman's sexuality entails much more than having physical sex. These seven components of sexuality—life wisdom, intimacy, sensuality, physical sexuality, body image, sexual identity, medical matters—make it more complicated than simply making love. And ultimately more beautiful.

The Seven Wedges of Sexuality

The Wheel of Sexuality is based on a survey of women who have attended **Sex on the Porch**. It shows by proportion the topics that have affected their sexuality most as seasoned women. These topics make up the seven wedges, which are discussed one by one.

Wedge #1 – Life Wisdom

What has shaped your sexuality as a woman? Have you wondered why you think dramatically differently than your best friend (or even your own daughter!) about intimate behavior and attitudes toward men? Have you thought, "How can she say/do/think *that*?" You've learned "how to be a sexual woman" from a lifetime of unique sexual experience different than hers. Some experiences supported your positive growth as a woman; others may have spiraled you into a chasm of fear leading to years of defensive posturing.

To illustrate, at a young age, you might have witnessed a man

WHEEL OF SEXUALITY:
Seasoned, Sexy Woman at *Sex on the Porch*™

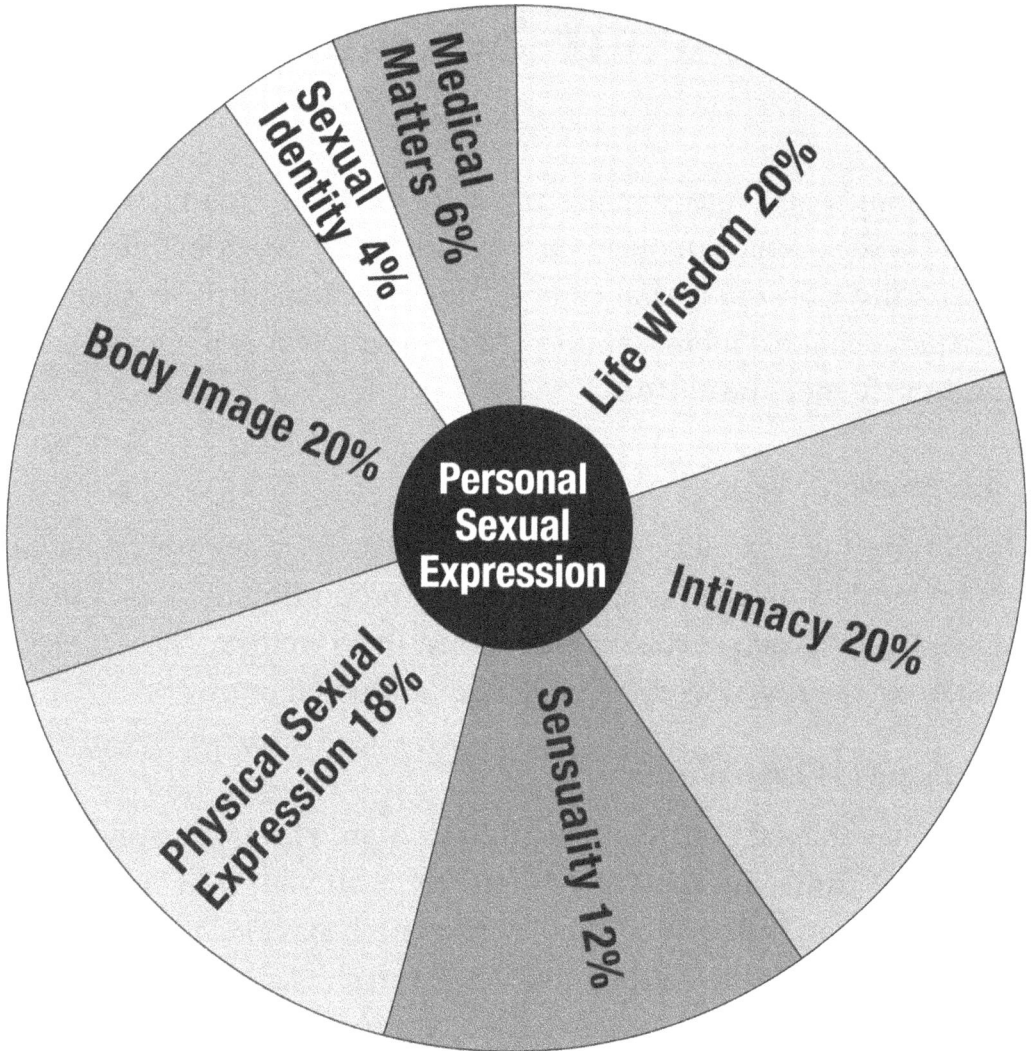

Medical Matters 6%

Sexual Identity 4%

Body Image 20%

Life Wisdom 20%

Personal Sexual Expression

Intimacy 20%

Physical Sexual Expression 18%

Sensuality 12%

exposing himself to you against your will (not talked about, but sadly, it frequently happens to young girls). On the other hand, you might have had a first sexual experience with a gentle, kind, passionate guy who cared deeply about your satisfaction and happiness. I know of one woman who had been told by consecutive teenage boyfriends that she was too fat. Today, this stunningly attractive woman sees herself as heavy and unworthy. Conversely, another friend carries herself beautifully in her larger frame, in part because she had grandparents who told her continually how lovely she was, inside and out.

Highlights from Sex on the Porch

Julianne, 71, told us how she was introduced to sex education. She said, "I went to a strict Catholic school. One day—I guess it was in eighth grade—I walked into our girls-only health class, and the nuns had written SEX EDUCATON in big, bold letters on the blackboard in red chalk. Naturally, at our age, we felt nervous and eager at the same time. Then Sister Mary Catherine walked to the front of the class with a stack of newspapers. After handing every girl a newspaper, she instructed us to lay them on our laps, saying, 'Put the newspaper on the lap of every boy you go out with if he asks you to sit on his lap. That way, you won't get pregnant.' End of SEX ED lesson!

"You know, I carried a newspaper with me for years, even when I knew the idea was ridiculous. We're so impressionable as young women, especially when it comes to messages from people we respect."

We've lived a lifetime of experiences that flavor how we see ourselves today. While some of our former teachings are worth keeping, many need to be sent to the trash can. Other life experiences that influence how you see yourself as a sexual woman: ethnic values, traditional religious doctrine, friendships, treatment by former partners, and more. Yes, we bring a compendium of events with us to the table today. All of them influence how we present ourselves to the world as a seasoned, sexual woman.

What experiences do you bring from your childhood that still help you? Which ones can you let go?

Wedge #2 – Intimacy

Intimacy—feelings of closeness to another human being—is the foundation of personal relationships. As women, we are hard-wired with hormones that function as networking bridges. We naturally seek a connection with a partner before we proceed with any intimate or relationship liaison, whether it's spiritual, sexual, or simply casual.

"Women's intuition" is real; we just "know" if relationships are right. As sexual women, we enjoy an intensity of intimacy that most men simply do not have. We've honed our ability to listen to feelings that will usually lead us to the right connection. Every woman expresses her unique need for intimacy differently. Some are happy nurturing a few deep friendships; others need to be more intense with multi-layered connections; still others naturally seek passionate sexual bonds to get the level of intimacy they require. Whatever form it takes, intimacy is an essential part of who we are as women.

❧

Kat's Quips
Intimacy vs. Sex

Intimacy is the need to be emotionally close to another human being. Sex is the biological urge to make love. Stereotypically, most women can have intimacy without sex but rarely enjoy sex without intimacy. By comparison, most men can have sex with or without intimacy.

What do you need in an intimate relationship that's different now than at any other time in your life?

Wedge #3 – Sensuality

All five of our senses are deeply connected to *who we are* as sexual women. That makes paying attention to all five senses extremely important.

Sense of touch is what comes to mind immediately when we think about sexuality. We like to be hugged and held in certain ways that are special to us. Whether it's during lovemaking or it's a hand massage while having a manicure, each woman likes to be stroked and caressed in her own way.

The other four senses—sight, hearing, taste, and smell—are just as important as touch and beg for attention all day long. If you're feeling down, you might be suffering from sensory deprivation. Your nervous system is crying out for help. All day on the computer? Your brain craves sensory satisfaction other than what the computer monitor presents.

For our purposes here, sensual gratification means meeting the needs of all five senses. That includes dressing in an outfit that makes you feel attractive and happy. Maybe it's the way the fabric touches your skin or the cleavage that you show that adds up. Enjoy the sense of sexuality it gives you. Spray your body with your favorite perfume and engulf yourself with a delicious aroma. Play music that jolts you into a titillating memory, leaving you smiling as you recall a secret rendezvous. Indulge in a morsel of dark chocolate and let it take you into romance, poetry, delight.

If you can connect to your five senses—all five at once for total pleasure—in a way that lifts you up as the beautiful woman that you are, your mood will dramatically lift, too. And as your 'tude picks up, who knows what might happen?

Which of your senses needs attention today? What will you do about it?

~

Highlights from Sex on the Porch

Juana, 60, divulged that, the day after our last meeting, she wore her new leather boots to work, along with tights and a great-looking skirt. Clearly, our discussion of sensuality had catapulted her desire to feel more attractive, downright decadent. Such a sensuous treat it was to sniff that wonderful scent of new leather boots. She was admired by no fewer than six of her co-workers who commented on her fun mood and asked, "What's different?" Three of her women friends at the office complimented her on her sexy new boots. And because she was more open than ever to her senses, she felt beautiful all day long.

Wedge #4 – Physical Sexuality
("making love" or "sex" as we traditionally think of it)

Physical sexuality means using your body for sexual enjoyment. Indeed, physical changes cascade over us at 55, 65, 75. As one **Sex on the Porch** participant, Leanne, 62, said, "Even my old dildo doesn't fit anymore!"

The tsunami of physical changes includes:

- You don't lubricate vaginally as much as you did before menopause. (This can be fixed with a good lubricant.)

- Intercourse might be painful. (That too can be treated.)

- Physically, everything just sags.

And your point is …? Yes, dramatic things take place! However, there are very few legitimate reasons—other than what's going on in your head—to deny yourself a great sex life in whatever way is best for you.

If you engage with a partner, mix it up! Tell him or her what you like and what you don't like. Consider all these benefits of regular sexual activity:

- Sex is good for your heart (literally and figuratively). Hormones that flood your body during sexual activity boost your immune system and provide a sense of calm.

- Orgasm floods your system with hormones that encourage healing and strengthen your pelvic floor.

- Sex gives your sagging body image a lift while increasing your self-confidence and self-esteem.

- Sex wards off depression

- Sex affirms that you're a beautiful, sensual women.
- Sex is recession proof; it's FUN and it's FREE!

We'll explore a variety of new activities to enjoy in the bedroom in Part II. For now, open yourself to new ideas! This is the time of your life for new adventures.

Where are you "stuck" in your bedroom that might require new thinking to enjoy your sexual adventures?

❧

Kat's Quip
Clitoris = Pleasure

Do you know that sex experts can find no good reason for the existence of the human female clitoris other than pleasure? Not to mention that we have tons more nerve endings in our clitoris than a man has in his penis.

Knowing that, let's celebrate, own it, and enjoy it!

Turns out that for all the male vibrato about sex, women are blessed with equipment that allows a much deeper and more profound pleasure than men experience.

Wedge #5 – Body Image

The pressures in this youth-dominated culture to look young can be demoralizing and devastating. On the other hand, we live in time of medical and spiritual knowledge that gives us new ways of thinking. Today, we can make psychological and medical choices that weren't available to former generations.

Both men and women suffer with body image issues like sagging faces and drooping bellies, though women get hit hardest. The fountain of youth doesn't exist, but the fountain of confidence and wisdom and beauty does. What's the key ingredient? Knowing *how to think about ourselves* as our bodies age. Confidence and wisdom can win out in the long run! (Part III tackles body image in detail.)

What fears about body image are getting in the way of regarding yourself as a beautiful woman? What can you do about it?

Wedge #6 – Sexual Identity

Sexual identity is much more than Lesbian, Straight, Gay, Bi-sexual, and Transsexual. Beyond those sexual orientations, sexual identity refers to how we actually elect to present ourselves to the world. Our personal presentation is as unique as a snowflake design; no two are the same. Tomboy, feminine, coy, fluffy, conservative, wild, buttoned-up, proper, butch, cougar, sophisticated, beautiful, natural, cute, masculine, motherly, business-like, bejeweled, plain, sexy. Which descriptions suit you? In which combination?

Who cares about your sexual identity? You do. Why should you care? To know and appreciate your singular expression of womanhood helps you understand why your life is unfolding as it is. Are you playing the role of who *you* think you should be, or are you trying to be something for someone else?

If you're feeling exhausted and unsure of yourself, you may be out of alignment with your authentic self. Millions of women in their 50s, 60s, 70s, and beyond attest to what Lucy, 78, said at **Sex on the Porch**: "I finally cracked and started over because I needed to be who I really am."

The most important role you'll ever play is to project the woman you *want to be*, not the woman who someone else tells you to be. That's critical to your life happiness. Right now, put away any magazines, websites, and feedback that suggest how you *should* be. None of that! This is about you alone, your true "shoes-off" self.

Are you being YOU? Are you living your life as that person? If not, what can you do differently?

❧

Titillating Tips
Answer this question ...

Are you really YOU?

To help my clients sort out this question, I have them make a list of five adjectives five times. They're instructed to write down the following:

1. The top five adjectives you'd use to describe *who you really are at your core* (e.g., tomboy, feminine, coy, fluffy, conservative, wild, buttoned-up, proper, butch, cougar, sophisticated, beautiful, natural, cute, masculine, motherly, business-like, bejeweled, plain, sexy, etc.). This helps you value yourself first.

2. The top five adjectives your parents would describe as you.

3. The top five adjectives from a spouse or partner as he/she sees you.

4. The top five adjectives your best friends use to describe you.

5. The top five adjectives your co-workers say about you.

Then we compare all five of the lists and look for differences. The gaps discovered explain the points of stress. This helps you present yourself to others in a way that reflects the authentic identity you value as a woman.

Wedge #7 – Medical Matters

As women in our 50s and beyond, we face everything from STIs, to yeast infections, to estrogen that skips all over the map during menopause, to vaginas that stretch out, shrink back, and get dry. We have breasts that get pulled and tugged for mammograms and suffer all degrees of cancers (most of which can be cured today if found in their early stages).

All this tells us that we need to know our way around our bodies.

What do you need to ask your medical specialist (including MD, chiropractor, acupuncturist, naturopath, etc.) that you haven't asked about sexuality?

❧

Highlights from Sex on the Porch

Stephanie, a first-timer with our **Sex on the Porch** group, broke into the tête-à-tête with urgency. She had been too embarrassed to ask her doctor about "this rash and burning sore down there." But the burning became unbearable, so she boomeranged back to the doctor (her family doctor, male) the next day. Diagnosis? Genital herpes. She was mortified. "Me?" she asked. "I don't sleep around! I've been married for 17 years. It's not fair. I have *no idea* where this came from!" (Genital herpes and HPV—human papilloma virus—can lie dormant for a long time, sometimes up to 25 years, before the virus produces symptoms.) Stephanie's experience is not unusual. Doctors today are inundated with so much information, so little time, and so much pressure from insurance companies that they hardly have time to do what they do best: practice medicine. *Never mind having time to educate patients about sex!*

❧

Titillating Tips
Talk to the doc!

Here's a wise phrase that's been around a while: *If it's to be, it's up to me.* And it's absolutely true. When things don't seem right "down there," it falls on your shoulders to ask questions. You need to rise above any embarrassment you might feel. If you have trouble articulating your problem, write it down and read it to the doctor. Doctors may not ask about your sex life (most don't), but they need to know certain details to give you a complete plan of care. It's up to you to step up to the plate and tell them so you can get the level of care required.

By the way, you have the right to find a new doctor if your current doctor doesn't answer your questions to your satisfaction. You know that, of course, but it's worth a reminder.

CHAPTER 3

Get a
Second Wind

Get a handle on what you want, what you already have, and what you need to be a sexually seasoned woman. Take a moment and complete this chart by checking the boxes that apply to you.

ELEMENTS OF YOUR LIFE INVOLVING INTIMACY AND SEXUALITY	Perfectly happy with the status quo	Okay but need to make changes	Very unhappy and must make improvements; my self esteem is at stake
My partner			
The type of men I am dating			
My home – a place where I feel safe			
My sex life with my life partner			
Activities I enjoy doing sexually			
My confidence level as a woman in bed			
My sex life when dating			
My sex life by myself			
Messages "from the grave" – what I learned about being a woman as a child			
My clothing as it reflects me as a woman			

ELEMENTS OF YOUR LIFE INVOLVING INTIMACY AND SEXUALITY	Perfectly happy with the status quo	Okay but need to make changes	Very unhappy and must make improvements; my self esteem is at stake
My body			
My friendships as a support for me			
My groups and associations that reflect who I am			
My work as it reflects my true talents			
My sexual identity is in sync with how I express myself as a woman			
My "bucket list" – special activities I want to do in my life as a sexual, sensual			
My medical concerns about my sexuality have been addressed			

Action List

What needs your attention from the list above? What do you need to adjust, energize, change, or eliminate? Make your list here:

_____

_____

_____

_____

_____

_____

_____

This *gift* of sexuality—this part of ourselves that gives us womanhood—can be a source of joy throughout our years on earth, no matter what has happened earlier in our lives or what we may face in the future.

If we look at our sexuality in healthy ways, it can be the essential element that keeps us fully alive, vital, and savoring the entire journey. Here's the deal: Sex, sexuality, and sexual expression are supposed to be fun for a lifetime. If that's not true in your life, make improvements now—those you noted on your Action List.

Now it's time for new possibilities! Part II provides a menu of delicious choices for expressing yourself sexually as a seasoned woman. Get ready to enjoy the ride.

Part Two

AM I NORMAL?

*P*art II explores new possibilities in the bedroom. Open yourself up to new ideas! This is the time of your life for new adventures.

What's the great news about the bedroom at midlife and beyond? You can do whatever you want to do—and "whatever you want" becomes "normal" for you. It means you never have to "perform" or stay stuck in the same old patterns.

These scenarios describe just a few possibilities:

- He wants bright lights so he can watch her body and himself.
- She feels sexy, sensual, slippery, and aroused by seeing shadows in the candlelight.

- He likes to watch himself move in front of a mirror.

- She likes pleasuring herself with the removable showerhead.

- He gets turned on wearing her panties.

- She likes to be tied up.

- They like to play pirate and prisoner blindfolded and have anal sex.

- Neither focuses on finding her G spot; rather, they're focused on pleasure.

- All of these describe *normal* sexual play—but not necessarily *average*.

CHAPTER 4

What's Normal?
What's Not Normal?

Normal is any sexual or intimate activity you might enjoy that doesn't hurt you or someone else, physically or psychologically. *Normal* is anything that's fun and titillating *for you*. It resonates with you; you simply don't care what other people are doing or thinking.

In contrast, *average* is the boring statistic that tells you what most people do in what frequency. *Average* means worrying about meeting a standard based on anonymous surveys, yet those surveys mislead us to judge ourselves as either "fitting in" or "not fitting in." Besides, studies have come and gone, and you still can't convince me that people tell the truth about sex when taking a survey.

Know that your seasoned sexual happiness is based on what uniquely appeals to you, not what turns others on. You *never* have to measure your seasoned sexual happiness by other people's opinions of what is sexy. Seasoned sex means you have a whole compendium of choices and life wisdom to help you satisfy your curiosity, your creativity, your libido, and your decisions. You can mix it up!

My advice? Throw away *average*. Pitch all the surveys that spit out how much, what kind, and how often; they establish *average* sex. And who wants *average* sex, anyway? Just wad up those magazine surveys and toss them into the recycle bin. Done. Now we can get to the real nitty gritty: *Are you getting what you want?*

Normal, "Most People," and You

Defining *normal* for "most people" at midlife and beyond becomes a moot question. Why? Because *normal* is impossible to measure. For example, a 66-year-old female client who chaired the church youth education committee seemed as pure as a white lace doily. Yet, behind closed doors, she yearned to be tied up and whipped by her dominating partner dressed in a black leather harness. Despite it being *normal* for her, was she likely to speak out about her preference for bondage and discipline, thus risking her position in the community? *I don't think so!* You can't tell by looking at people and guessing, believe me.

Let's imagine a chart that demonstrates what's *normal* for most people over 55. It would look ridiculous—something like this:

Activity	Is this normal for most people?
Intercourse	Probably, but sometimes not.
Oral sex – fellatio (oral stimulation of male genitals)	Depends. Maybe.
Oral sex – cunnilingus (oral stimulation of female genitals)	Yes and no.
Anal sex	Some couples love it; others are repulsed by it
Holding hands	You would think so but sometimes not.
Spanking	More than you would think.
Nipple clamps	Who can tell? Maybe.

This shows us we can't quantify *normal* for "most people," especially those in the second half of life. Besides, we've likely spent the first half of life doing what's *right*. Now in our later years, we can look at what feels *normal* to us.

Remember, what's *normal* differs for every couple, every individual. Fantasies, cravings, fetishes, dreams, positions, play, paths to arousal, even degrees of pressure—all vary for each person. It's also impossible to measure by those Great American Comparison Games called *What Is Everybody Else Doing?* and *What's Normal For Everyone Else?* It doesn't matter!

Identifying what's normal and what's abnormal for each of us as individuals, however, is not only possible; it's *imperative*. Why? It's like satisfying hunger with preferences for the foods we select and our schedule for eating. Think of sexual energy as a root force, a hunger, that gets satisfied with certain preferred actions at certain times.

Yes, everyone is different. If you're a vegetarian and your partner offers you prime rib, you won't appreciate it, and you may even be repulsed. But if your partner offers you a curried lentil ravioli, you may savor it and call it heavenly. (By the way, one sensible solution to mismatched desire is using the communication techniques addressed in Chapter 8 on page 117, "What to do if …".)

At midlife and beyond, it's vital to open up to new items on the sexual menu. Take time to explore new options for a better selection. For both sexes, the latest body change may require giving up trying Olympic-style sex positions. Reality hits: Many men lose the rock hard erections they had as 25 year olds and most post-menopausal women experience dryness in their vaginas, even when they feel aroused.

Is that bad news? Not necessarily. When one door closes, another (better one) opens. If we let go of the need to look and act 35 years old, the drive for sexual *performance* gives way to seeking sexual *pleasure*. And the *new normal* can include more fun, more adventure, and more exploration than ever before.

CHAPTER 5

"Normal" Activities Selection List

Look at the activities on the Sexual Selection List. Which would you like to become *normal* for you? Some of them might already be on your menu of choices; some might be alluring to try; some might actually disgust you.

Remember this:

- All of them are *normal* for some individuals.
- None of them are prerequisites to sexual happiness.
- Each of them is a choice, a preference, a menu item.
- No one choice is better than any other.
- They fit into the Golden Rule of Sex at Midlife Plus—*seek pleasure, not performance.*

Go ahead. Broaden your horizons. Open your thinking. You might not go for every single activity listed here, but reading them through might raise a "hmmmm." If a certain choice repulses you, then know that it's not your thing. *That's perfectly okay.* You want to recognize your comfort zone and spot new ideas to explore or fantasize about.

By the way, did you know that the brain has difficulty distinguishing between the real and the imagined? That's why fantasy works so well when having sex! If you are single (or a very private person in a partnership) and you can't or don't want to participate in the real world, you can allow your daydreams and personal pleasuring to take you into a fantasy world. That's *normal*, too.

❧

Kat's Quip
Try something new ...

Give yourself permission to try something new from the sexual selection list in this chapter. After all, you're a sexy seasoned woman.

Sexual Selection List

You'll find each activity discussed in more detail following this list.

The Usual Suspects (pgs. 44–61):

1. Traditional Old Standby: Intercourse

2. Time-honored Starter: Kissing

3. Touch: Helping hands

4. Going Down: Oral sex

More Exploration (pgs. 61–85):

5. Back Door: Anal sex

6. Sex Toys: Vibrators, dildos, and nipple clamps

7. Role-Playing: Grown-ups playing doctor, nurse, etc.

8. Fetishes: Food, leather, balloons, and more

9. Voyeurism/Exhibitionism: Love to watch and have to show

Not to Be Left Out (pgs. 86–101):

10. BDSM: Bondage, discipline, sado-masochism

11. Celibacy: The decision to abstain

12. Body Changes: Low libido, dry vagina, and other

13. Enhancers: Food, chocolate, drugs, alcohol, and more

ACTIVITIES 1 – 4

The Usual Suspects: Intercourse, Kissing, Touch, Oral Sex

1. INTERCOURSE

The king of the list—or so we were taught. Personally, I'd like to dethrone this one. It sits at the top of the list because we've been conditioned in younger years to define *sex and lovemaking* as strictly intercourse (or a good "fuck"). Newsflash: There are lots of other ways to have a darn good time and make love, too.

Most of us grew up expecting that sexual activity isn't complete without intercourse. For us today, that's nonsense! But in our earlier years, intercourse was the Big Kahuna in lovemaking for these reasons:

- Desire to procreate
- Raging hormones
- Pressure to perform (for both men and women)
- Proving one's stamina
- Limited knowledge about sexual technique and the opposite sex

Honestly, intercourse simply isn't as popular as you might think with the seasoned crowd because the reasons listed here tend to disappear at midlife and beyond. Many people I know seldom or never opt for the BIG "I."

Nonetheless, some male clients say they still want the BIG "I" to be the main course. Give it up, guys. Have you ever asked a woman how she feels about it? Truth told, many mature women appreciate not being "pounded," and men are so much happier when they learn that the "performance" requirement of younger years can give way to pleasure *in other ways* for their partner. Everyone exhales.

Imagine. If partners take the time to talk and explore, they find out that the BIG "I" doesn't have to be the *piece de resistance* it has been.

❧

Highlights from Sex on the Porch

Through our anonymous question box at **Sex on the Porch**, one participant (I still don't know who submitted this) told us that she and her husband— both in their 60s and married 35 years—*rarely* have intercourse AND they have great sex several times a week.

How can this be? Creativity and a sense of adventure! Their favorite is oral sex on each other, but they also stay open to new ideas by wandering through sex toy stores together.

❧

Titillating Tips
Getting it up with the blue pill

A note about sildenafil citrate (Viagra®), Tadalafil (Cialis®), and Vardenafil (Levitra®).

Although some men can use these phospho-diesterase (PDE) inhibitors successfully, most seasoned men don't actually need them. Why? Because our biggest sex organ is the brain, not a huge penis. And the brain determines erections, not the chemicals that come from specific drugs.

So if a man decides he can't get erect without the drugs … guess what? He won't! If he goes to Hawaii for his honeymoon and forgets his Viagra®, chances are he'll feel nervous. What follows? Self-conscious lovemaking and "iffy" erections. However, if he decides that getting an erection as huge and hard as a 25 year old doesn't matter—and his partner likes exploring other avenues to great sex—he may surprise himself with an unintended extra-hard erection.

Even better, he (and his partner) won't be disappointed if the erection doesn't happen at all. Besides, many men can't take Viagra® et al because of other medications, or the drug flat out doesn't work for them.

Here's the point: Taking a little blue pill isn't a panacea. It's better to seek pleasure through new possibilities. These pills do not account for passion, desire, or intimacy. An erection does not equal intimacy in which caring, loving, and affection occur. (*Tip:* Just because a man over 50 doesn't get an erection, it doesn't mean he's not aroused. Men can ejaculate without an erection.)

The answer to the question "what do you like?" suggests that, at midlife-plus, partners can make lovemaking fun in ways that doesn't always involve vaginal penetration. So, women, take the pressure off men to "perform." Investigate new possibilities. Consider exploration a privilege of age and wisdom. After all, being highly creative shows high intelligence.

Now, I'm not suggesting that you omit having intercourse if you enjoy it. If the BIG "I" has always been your focus, then think variety, creativity, and *comfort.*

Yes, comfort. No more extreme positions. Let's give our bodies and our psyches a break! Let the extreme positions go—from extremely boring (missionary) to extremely difficult (legs wrapped around standing up). Instead, find a position that is hot, sexy, and *easy*. If he is comfortable standing and you are comfortable lying on the bed, try this great position: Get it on with him standing up facing the side of the bed and you lying horizontally across it. Your hips are on the edge of the bed, legs up, exposed to him. He penetrates you at the edge of the bed, and you can swing your legs up on his chest. Penetration feels great to you both, and all hands are on deck, free to play with your clitoris during his thrusts and wander to any number of thrilling places!

Sure, make intercourse a menu item, but only one of many choices. And when you do, get rid of those "so very yesterday" positions. Simply rely on your own imaginations!

❧

Titillating Tips
If you must "do it"—two non-negotiables for intercourse

1. Use lots of lubrication to make penetration more comfortable for you. Just do it. After menopause, most women simply don't lubricate well so forget about your natural juices. The degree of moistness no longer signifies how turned on you are. Use a high-quality water-based lube only. Nothing sugar-based or petroleum-based. Certainly no petroleum jelly. I have searched the world over for the best lubes. My favorite lubrication is *Slippery Stuff*. (You can discreetly order it on my website: www.getasecondwind.com.) It's well researched, water based, no harsh chemicals, and has no aftertaste during oral sex.

2. If you're not *absolutely* certain that your partner is free from sexually transmitted infections, you *must* use a condom. Long-term monogamous partners may be excused from this mandate, but everyone else is subject to strict enforcement. *The condom police will get you!* Seriously, get tested, then carry your papers with you. No papers = no partner, and no penetration. *Be strict and inflexible about this with any potential partner.*

2. KISSING

Many women like active tongues and deep tongue-down-your-throat kisses. Some like open-mouth kissing with deep breaths coming in and out during the kiss. Others prefer keeping their lips closed. Then there are women who want to kiss and be kissed all over their bodies—and their opposites who say "lips off of me" no matter where.

What do *you* prefer? Think about it. Determine what you like and don't like when it comes to kissing. Then tell your partner.

In fact, lots of people don't like kissing. They consider it messy, germy, sloppy, smelly. I know one husband and wife who have been making love for 25 years. They haven't kissed romantically since their wedding night because they find it disgusting. That's *normal* for them.

Yes, you can experience great sex without kissing. On the other hand, intimate kissing can be the highlight of a sexual interlude if that's what you like. I know a man who gets a giant hard-on at the mere thought of having her lips on his. He's 72, by the way.

3. TOUCH: HELPING HANDS

Your hands can be hot little helpers. Again, take a personal inventory of what you enjoy. Don't assume you *should* like being touched in certain ways. Some women don't like their breasts touched; others say "hands off" on any number of areas—tummies, thighs, feet, ears, butts, necks, and more. Again, everyone is different. And *normal*.

Consider these activities that hands can do and decide where they might fit into your menu selection:

- *Holding hands:* Everyone loves it, right? Not true. Some people get turned off by public displays of affection but might act like rebels behind closed doors.

- *Massage:* Touch is necessary to human survival. Some people crave all-over-body caresses; some run from them. Clothes on or off is a-okay. Again, everyone's different. If you've never had a massage by a professional, try it. But first let the person know if you feel hesitant. Some people like "happy endings" (an actual term used by the erotic massage industry). It's a genital orgasm provided by the masseuse or masseur. Don't worry; if you don't ask for it, the masseuse or masseur won't offer it. Know that therapeutic massage therapists (those who work at spas) would be highly offended if you asked for a happy ending. Behind your own private closed doors with your partner, however, go for it—if it feels *normal* to you.

- *Tickling and/or pinching:* Scary torture for some, hot bondage techniques for others, fun flirting for many, detested by a few. All *normal.* The laughing stems from your central nervous system, not because it appeals to your sense of humor, by the way.

- *Hand jobs:* I'm hard pressed to find any woman who doesn't go for this gift from a partner, although there are a few women who don't want to be manually touched "down there." For men and women who enjoy genital caressing, talented hands have brought more pleasure than the purple-headed warrior ever dreamed of by himself, although for some, using the head of a penis to rub on the clitoris can cause an explosion of an orgasm.

Try doing this while standing up or standing above him with him seated in a chair. Straddle the chair and hold on to the shaft of his penis, and rub the head over your clitoris. Add lots of lubricant to your fingers and the vulva area, making the slippery-slidy effect pure bliss for both. Slather it all over—no time for neatness. Bonus feature: Unlike dildos and vibrators, your hands never run out of batteries and have built-in controls, including all degrees of pressure, width, motion, touch. Nothing else on the market beats it—yet.

- *Masturbation:* If you don't do it already, start! Is this *normal*? You bet! It's not easy for everyone, however. Sadly, I've known many women in my groups who are terrified of touching themselves erotically "down there." If you received the guilt messages as a child about touching yourself, then analyze exactly who and what that message was about. Perhaps, your parents were protecting themselves from the remote possibility that you might touch yourself inappropriately in public and, heaven forbid, embarrass them. Let's face it, our parents had their own unresolved guilt trips about who-knows-what—religion, etiquette, sex—leading to fear, shame, misinformation. Good news! That was then, this is now. It's time to enjoy your body! I'm convinced that our creator made our arms just long enough so that we can easily reach that pleasure zone between our legs.

  ~ My prescription for women: Masturbate once a week (at least), especially around and past menopause. If you can masturbate to reach orgasm, wonderful. If not, it's just fine to enjoy the ripples of pleasure that laying a hand on yourself can do. Call it whatever you wish that gives you permission to have a great time: self-pleasuring, understanding your body, playing with yourself, pat the bunny, polish the car, laying on of hands. Just do it!

~ If your fingers don't do it for you, use a vibrator or any other object that feels good to you. One favor: Be sure it's clean and big and solid enough that it can't break into pieces or get stuck up in your vagina if you push it in too far. No doubt you've heard emergency room stories about the removal of something "up there." If you think it was embarrassing at age 22, imagine how you would feel at age 72? And it's a big "duh" to assert that you put nothing breakable, no glass inside, isn't it?

~ What *is* the big deal about masturbation or self-pleasuring? It has magnificent benefits. Let me count the ways:

(1) It's a gift from your body to you. It teaches you that your amazing body can respond to you in all times of crisis, joy, love, and sadness. It feels good! And sometimes, when nothing else feels good, loving yourself is certainly nice.

(2) It's a huge stress reliever. Why? Because during orgasm, you get flooded with oxytocin, the feel-good hormone of contentment.

(3) It allows you to discover *how* you want to be touched—and how you *don't* want to be touched— so you can teach your partner. Feel free to touch

everything on your body and experiment. Play with your breasts, your face, your ears, your face, your genitals the way you like to! Some women find playing with their feet to be a turn on, too. It's all *normal*, and it's all okay.

(4) No one has to know you're masturbating. It's private (unless you opt to offer your partner an eyeful of fun watching you. For some partners, that's a real turn on). You can even play with all those toys you've wanted to try—and no one has to know. If you feel embarrassed walking into a store, just let me know and I will get them for you (contact me at info@getasecondwind.com)

(5) At midlife, keeping the body tuned up is important—and masturbation does that for your genitals. When you work out at the gym, your large body muscles stay in shape. Same drill with your pelvic floor during your at-home self-pleasuring workout. As you get aroused, your natural lubrication keeps the vagina well oiled. Feel free to add your own lube from a tube, as well. Hip thrusting exercises your perineum muscles, not to mention your heart rate goes up as you get aroused. Plus personal private sexual expression hastens healing and reduces pain.

(6) Here's how to masturbate: Cup your hand gently over your clitoris area—on top or inside the lips is fine—and just enjoy the sensation without moving. Simply hold your hand there. Learn to feel safe with that sensation first. Then get out the

lube and put it on yourself (after first warming it up in the palm of your hand). Move your fingers gently around. Notice what feels good and what does not. Find your clitoris and gently massage it. Take your time. Orgasm is not the goal. Simply *feeling good* is the goal.

(7) Can't allow yourself to touch yourself erotically? Let me be direct here—it's time to get past that. See a counselor like myself who understands the challenges you face when "letting go" of your prejudices about self-pleasuring. When you do, you'll bring a truly satisfying activity into your life.

❦

Highlights from Sex on the Porch

Betsy, 64, a partnered lesbian, came to **Sex on the Porch** with two specific questions: Is it possible that my partner is using masturbation to take the place of real sexual expression? And is she addicted to it?

At night, when Betsy goes into the bedroom where her partner is already in bed, lights are out and it's quiet. However, Betsy can hear her partner moaning as she approaches the bedroom, then sudden silence when she walks into the room. She's worried that this goes on during the day as well since her partner is unemployed and possibly depressed. And yes, their sex life together is "in the tank."

Is she addicted to masturbation? Well, yes and no. First, I think it's wise to avoid labeling activities we don't understand as addictions. Betsy worries that her partner is spending too much time alone with her vibrator. Meanwhile, her partner feels vulnerable and alone, no doubt suffering from the insecurities of being unemployed and being turned down after multiple interviews. Because Betsy's partner is looking for security and stability, she seeks that through self-pleasuring. Her body gives her those feelings to some degree.

Is it the right course of action? It's a stop gap until the couple can have a gentle conversation about pleasuring each other, especially during this stressful time.

❧

Kat's Quips
Can masturbation be an addiction?

Masturbation becomes an addiction when it interferes with life's daily tasks or when it stands in the way of a healthy relationship for a couple. Often, having an honest discussion of needs and concerns can divert attention away from substituting masturbation for mutual pleasuring. If an addiction is clearly present, counseling may be needed.

However, understanding that masturbation is a natural manner of tension release goes miles to relax everyone involved about having an addiction. After a couple has an initial conversation that expresses genuine concern, I might suggest masturbating together. Mutual masturbation can be a new activity to add spice to a sexual relationship.

~ *Do midlife-plus men need to masturbate?* Yes. Statistics say that men masturbate more than women, but no one really knows that to be true. And really, it makes no difference. Men are hard-wired to ejaculate. They do it in their sleep and almost all men do it to themselves when they're awake with a few exceptions (but not many). That's normal for them, too, by the way. Some women consider it hot to watch their partners masturbate (it's part of their sexual routine) while others don't want to know about it.

In any case, common sense suggests that males in their 50s, 60s, and beyond are wise to put a hand to their penises frequently. Regular masturbation actually *decreases* the chance of prostate cancer. It makes sense. The prostrate is a gland that needs liquid passing through it or it stagnates. Get your partner a tube of great lube and help him out.

Again, some women will love that idea and others want nothing to do with it. Both responses are normal.

• *Spanking:* Have you been a bad girl? Has your partner been bad? Well, then, you (or he) need to be punished (all in play, of course). Our childhood experience with this hands-on activity often dictates whether it's a sexual turn-on or not. It can work both ways. If getting a spanking was scary and awful as a little girl, this can be a gentle way to get past those old memories. For some, flirting with the threshold of pain can be exciting and sexually arousing. For others, a slap on the bottom can bring back memories of humiliation—an immediate turn off. Sometimes one partner prefers it and the giver happily goes along with that preference. But be sure to discuss spanking as a sexual activity; both partners must agree that it's good for them. While enjoying an intimate interlude, if your partner spanks you, tell him if you don't like it. You can gently say, "That doesn't work for me."

4. ORAL SEX

Licking, kissing, and sucking your partner's genitals is a mainstream activity. But is it *normal*? Yes, if you enjoy it. And it's normal to *not* like it, too.

Some women love it all—getting and giving—making oral sex pleasurable for them. Others enjoy bestowing it on their partners but not receiving it. All *normal*.

Truth told, many people prefer a good licking to a good poke! In fact, oral sex is the #1 favorite among the over-50 men and women I interviewed. Yes, for both men and women. It seems that the higher the age, the more interest they have in oral sex.

The tongue itself—what an amazing tool—offers these amazing features, it:

- allows one partner to be the center of attention and get pleasured by the other partner without distractions.

- provides a built-in, always-available lubricant.

- feels soft and erotic, both if you're the giver and the receiver.

- takes pressure off men because it doesn't require rock hard erections (and possible disappointment if erections don't happen).

- affords women who don't reach orgasm easily a situation in which they can concentrate without distraction—and possibility experience orgasm. (Needs to be said here: Reaching orgasm is not essential to enjoying good sex!)

However, "giving head" and/or "being eaten out" disgusts some people. Words women have used to describe why they won't participate in oral sex include germs, unclean, nasty taste, degrading, humiliating. Yes, it's all in how your brain interprets it. For them, oral sex is not normal. (*Tip:* About male organ cleanliness: Actually, being "unclean" is usually not true unless the male partner is uncircumsized and smegma—the white substance sometimes called "cheese"—gathers under the foreskin, creating an odor. In that case, every woman in the world has the right to tell him to wash up before her mouth will wrap itself around his throbbing member!)

Ladies, listen up. While being pleasured by him, keep these points in mind:

- Expect your guy to lose his erection when he's licking your genitals. Don't take it personally. He'll get it back.

Allow him the luxury of working on you and letting sensations of pleasure come up for you.

- Tell him what you like and don't like. Otherwise, believe me, he is guessing. Unless you clue him in, pleasuring a woman with oral sex is one of the biggest mysteries of the universe to a man. When he does something you like, a simple response like "I like that" will do. If he's grinding away with too much pressure or if his beard scratches you, tell him that, too. If you'd like more pressure from him, say, "Ooooh, that feels good. You can do that harder."

- Note that it's not *only* your clitoris that brings you to orgasm (although for most women, that's primarily what needs stimulation). It might be hot for you to have him lick the ridges of your vulva and the opening to your vagina. Sometimes the side-to-side movement of shaking his head while licking you brings on arousal more than tongue motion alone. Then again, maybe not. Everyone is different.

- Although some women don't orgasm with oral sex, many do. Nothing right or wrong about it either way. If you want to come and can't using tongue action alone, combine the use of your or his fingers with the tongue's activity. Or alternating a vibrator with the tongue action can work, too. If you can't orgasm at all during oral sex, no worries. Experiment with other ways to come such as using a vibrator or hand action. Remember, everyone is different. Some women barely need to be touched, and they come. Others need the pressure of industrial-strength car polishers to come. Both are *normal*.

- Rumor has it that the upper left quadrant of the clitoris (as you look down at it, or upper right for your partner facing it) is the most sensitive area. Never been proven, but I've known many women who agree.

Ladies, when you are pleasuring him orally, know this:

- For men, the head of the penis and the juncture of the head with the shaft are usually the most sensitive areas.

- He can ejaculate without an erection. Lack of knowledge around this little-known fact causes many a tired woman licking a soft organ to get frustrated and give up.

- Like you do, every man likes a different amount of pressure when he's touched. Be sure to ask your partner if the pressure you're using is right for him.

- Ask him to tell you about any motion he especially loves; don't pretend to know. Even couples in long-term relationships don't really know what their partners like. Ask! After all, if you were making dinner, you'd ask what food your partner would like to eat. This is no different.

- Sometimes men don't care if they come; other times they do care. Ask your partner. It's possible he may feel pressure to perform when he really doesn't want to.

- When it comes to swallowing "come" (often written "cum"), is it *normal*? (This refers to swallowing semen when a man ejaculates into a woman's mouth. When I say this, I can hear the "eeewwws" and "that's nauseating; that's repulsive." I can also hear the chorus of women sighing with relief that someone says doing this is okay, especially if they've been enjoying it for years.) Know this: There is nothing physically harmful about swallowing semen (provided your partner is clean from sexually transmitted infections or STIs). Semen is loaded with hormones and protein. No, I'm not recommending swallowing semen for its nourishment value. It simply can be a preference for women who enjoy it. The point is, don't let anyone coerce you into swallowing by saying, "It's what hot women do." Many women enjoy oral sex yet will have nothing to do with swallowing or having semen anywhere near their faces. Know that, if you feel comfortable with it and enjoy it, that's *normal*. It's also normal if the mere thought of doing it brings on nausea. Don't do it if it repulses you; he'll be just fine without it.

Titillating Tips
Something to know about "69"

It's tough to hold the position called "69" (lying facing each other with your head at his genitals and his head at your genitals) for very long. And few people actually orgasm when doing it. So if "69" is your goal, lie on your sides to pleasure each other. (It might be tough to get excited about having a penis and a set of testicles in your face, with him on top, let alone reach orgasm—although some women love it! Again, everyone is different.)

ACTIVITIES 5 – 9

More Exploration

The following five activities are also normal, although slightly further "out there" and still really fun.

5. ANAL SEX

More people than you ever would guess enjoy this. That doesn't mean you ever have to participate as either the giver or the receiver if you don't want to. It simply means that it's normal for many people. Nothing ugly about it unless you decide that it is. The anus and surrounds are highly sensitive and erogenous. Touching and gentle probing can be hot, hot, hot if you want to explore.

⌁

Highlights from Sex on the Porch

After someone asked if anal sex was normal, Patti shared that, on her last date, her new boyfriend pulled out this ominous-looking black cone-shaped *thing* about four inches long. A butt plug. It's carefully inserted it into the anus with lots of lubrication gel and rubber gloves on the hands of the inserter. Because the plug doesn't always go in easily at first, a hefty dose of patience might be required.

As I explained to the group, the receiver needs to relax so the sphincter muscle can open to let the butt plug in. Men find this sexy because of its constant pressure on the prostate gland, which tends to enlarge as they age. Women like it because the plug provides a sense of fullness and pressure that feels good in the same way it does when they push out a bowel movement. (Little kids like to hold back their "feces" for the same reason, by the way.) Some men and women are comfortable leaving the "butt plug" in while also enjoying intercourse. For others, it's uncomfortable, or they prefer each activity to be separate. Again, all of this is normal if it's your idea of fun. For others, it might not be appealing.

Looking around at **Sex on the Porch**, I saw giggling, rapt attention, rolling eyes, and one or two loud protests declaring, "No such exploits in my house!" Over in the corner, Julie sat feverishly working on her knitting. Ready to move on, I reached into our anonymous question box for the next question. Before I could ask it, though, Julie put down her knitting and calmly asked, "What's normal, Kat?" Genevieve blurted out, "*Not* a butt plug!" Titters everywhere.

Then Julie forged ahead. "But if you use a plug, you get poop on it, and that's not fun in the middle of having sex." Then she turned to me and repeated the original question, "Is anal sex normal, Kat?" Yes, it's absolutely *normal* and can be lots of fun, but only if you want it. By the way, getting "feces" on anal toys is part of the package in anal sex. It has to be handled discreetly and with attention to sanitation. Giving the receiver of anal sex a water enema before the activity will reduce the odds of feces being present. The penis is used for penetration; it goes without saying that a condom must sheath it. Rubber gloves must always be worn if fingers are used. Some women like to put condoms on anal toys, making sure the condoms don't come off. When toys are used, they must never be used again vaginally. After use, all anal activity toys must be washed in scalding water or boiled. Never use a toy that has not been thoroughly washed.

Here's the deal with anal sex:

- Always use lubricant and gloves. Never, never, never have anal sex without lots of lubrication! Sensitive tissues will tear, and you will have more problems than you bargained for. Although Vaseline® is good, any number of lubricants are made for this activity. Slippery Stuff, available on my website (www.getasecondwind.com) makes an excellent product that works well for anal sex. The lube job for the anus needs to be thicker than for lubricating the vagina. If you want to lick the anus, put a common plastic wrap like Saran™ Wrap between your tongue and your partner's anus. Your partner won't be able to tell the difference, no matter what he or she says. (And nor will you, for that matter.)

- Start the penetration extremely slowly. Whether you are the giver or the receiver, follow this instruction to avoid tearing tissues:

   (1) Circle the rim of the anus with a rubber-gloved finger doused in lubricant.

   (2) As your partner relaxes, insert one small finger into the rectum wearing a rubber glove that is dripping in lube. (Remember, use at least twice the lube you would use for vaginal lubrication.) Put lube on the glove and slather some around the

anus itself. The rectum has no lubricating device of its own. In fact, the rectum absorbs liquid and dries out the contents before depositing feces outside the body.

(3) When you feel ready for a dildo or a condom-sheathed penis to be inserted (i.e., the sphincter muscle has relaxed sufficiently), work in the inserted object gently. Take your time. Never insert any object farther than the length of an average erect penis (about five inches).

Anal sex is all about relaxing. It's impossible to do if you are nervous about it. If it takes you several attempts, and it's just not working, come back to it at another time. It can be erotic and pleasurable, but it can be nerve wracking if it doesn't please you. Don't ever force it. Take your time and know that it might take two or more attempts.

6. SEX TOYS: vibrators, dildos, nipple clamps, and other toys

Sex toys have become household words that were rarely (if ever) mentioned when we were children. Our sons and daughters, nieces and nephews have grown up with ads for them plastered all over the Internet. If you're lucky, your computer's spam filter gets rid of the "vibrator" ads for you. Yet toys such as vibrators can add to your pleasure. I consider them a mandatory part of every post-menopausal woman's toolkit. Your attitude toward them—and your willingness to experiment—will dictate whether they pleasure you or not.

❧

Titillating Tips
About vibrators and dildos and women in the second half of life

Listen up!

The modern post-menopause woman's closet should include at least one good vibrator (a battery-operated tool that vibrates and stimulates the vulvar area) and one good dildo (phallic-shaped object that goes into the vagina to simulate penetrative intercourse).

I contend that these ecstasy makers are essential at midlife and beyond. Like a microwave, your life can go on without having one. But there simply are times when they step in to perform a function that nothing else—not a tongue, not hands—can provide. A healthy supply of sex toys is "good for what ails ya'" as my mother used to say.

Sex advice columns espouse the virtues of fancy vibrators, dildos, and other toys with a plethora of labels from the ridiculous to the sublime. Ignore all the promises. Know this: A vibrator and dildo that are *basic* serve practical functions and they are enough. Refrain from buying the fancy products you'll likely never use. My motto: keep sex simple.

Some considerations about using sex toys:

- They're fun and titillating to use, with or without a partner. Nothing wrong with good clean fun!

- With sex toys, use lots of water-based quality lube (I recommend Slippery Stuff s noted at www.getasecondwind.com under "Products"). Slather it all over your vulva. Don't be shy; no one knows what you're doing except you (unless you want your partner to watch!). Because it's a water-based gel, not petroleum-based, don't worry about staining the sheets. Any marks will come out in the wash.

- For some women, a vibrator and/or dildo smoothes the way to having "the Big O" orgasm (if that's what you desire). For others, the movement just feels good and orgasm comes from other stimulation. (Yes, you can have lots of fun without pressuring yourself to "come." You can simply enjoy feeling oh-wowwww-sooo-good without an orgasm at the end.)

- Regular use of a good dildo and lubrication keeps women stretched out at a time when their vaginas tend to shrink. (Don't panic. Vaginas don't shrink *up* without the formerly abundant supply of estrogen; they just get smaller due to thinner walls. Good lubing prevents micro tears in the vaginal wall.)

- Maybe the best part is that playing with sex toys distracts you when you're feeling low or alone.

- Remember, exploring with a vibrator and/or dildo can teach you how to love your body and get creative without the pressure of a partner's attention. Yippee!

It can be awkward—even overwhelming—to select vibrators and dildos in a store or online. I suggest you first buy a dildo (fake penis, for lack of a better term) and then get a vibrator. Why? From my experience, it's best to experience the subtler sensation of a dildo first. We all know that penises don't vibrate inside you—that is, unless your male partner is wearing a vibrating "cuff" (a cuff fits over a penis to increase length and girth, and some of them vibrate). Furthermore, a dildo is gentler than a vibrator so you can listen to your body while exploring and sensing what you enjoy and don't enjoy. You can use the dildo to stimulate the clitoris much more tenderly than a vibrator would. Also, you won't be distracted by noise, vibration speed, getting it on the right spot, waiting for it to take you to orgasm, and other concerns.

About dildos (fake penises):

Remember that the average penis is 5½ inches erect. I suggest buying a dildo that's average size and avoid the temptation to get an anatomically correct giant "telephone pole" that promises to please every inch of your desire (available up to 10 inches!). Fuhgeddaboudit. Unless you know you can accommodate it vaginally (and if you can, you probably don't need this sexuality coaching), go for the 5½ inch average size, about 1¼ inches thick. That way, you can feel the fullness in your vagina and enjoy your ecstasy without any pain. If it hurts when you pull it out, change up. Buy the smallest size possible and gradually work your way up to the 5½-inch style. It may be that your vagina has shrunk—a normal and natural condition—and you need to gently encourage it to stretch.

Get a dildo with a flat base that can stand up by itself on your bedside table. Note these advantages:

- You can hold it with a better grip.
- It can't get sucked up into your vagina if you push it too far.
- You can sit on it during your private escapades.
- You can have your partner wear it in a "strap on" harness belt.

Don't rule out using a dildo. Our lesbian sisters have much to teach straight women about the use of harnesses, and they can be fun if you are open to using them. (*Note:* Harness belts or "strap ons" are simply a low-slung belt with an opening for a dildo. The dildo hangs from the belt in roughly the same angle as a penis hangs from a man's body.)

About vibrators:

You can find as many vibrators as there are women to buy them. The world of sex toys can be discombobulating! So start out with a basic model featuring several speeds and then build your inventory from there. Select for quality and your unique needs. (*Tip:* Buying a good vibrator without figuring out what you need is like buying a car without deciding what you want it to do for you. Know your own needs.)

How do you even know what pressure you want? What pressure do you prefer when you masturbate? Do you want a light touch? Do you massage extra hard? You'll find the degree of vibration all over the map in these products. Some women prefer industrial-strength vibration; others prefer a light touch with barely any vibration at all. It's important to know; using your vibrator on the wrong speed can fully ruin the experience.

Go to a sex toy shop and test the strength in your hand with samples, if available. If not, buy one online from a reputable source who provides an accurate description of the products. Whether it's a vibrator or a dildo you're buying, get high-quality plastic. (Almost all are made of plastic, by the way.) Please call or email me (info@ getasecondwind.com) and I will help you select the one that's good for you.

If you don't want to use a vibrator, that's okay—and that's *normal*! Maybe you find the vibration too strong or you just don't like the idea of using it. Your fingers can do the trick just fine.

⤜⤛

Kat's Quip
Give 'em a whirl …

Truth told, I consider dildos and vibrators akin to exercise and vegetables—that is, a necessary part of the second half of our life. If you've never used one or both, give 'em a whirl. You might find a new source of delight. And if they're already part of your daily diet, you go girl!

About nipple clamps:

Ouch or ooooyesss. Basically, nipple clamps are clothespins that clip on a woman's nipples. While some women love them, for others, it's like a mammogram during sex. Before the emergence of sex shops, clothespins did the trick. And really, that's all nipple clamps are: glorified clothespins.

Because the pleasure center in your breasts ties directly to your vulva area, it makes sense that pinching the nipples would arouse you. For some women, it works; for others, it doesn't. When your partner squeezes your nipples, does it turn you on? If so, you're a candidate for nipple clamps. However, experiment with clothespins before investing in fancy nipple clamps, or just pinch your nipples to test the feelings you experience. By the way, many men find nipple clamps stimulating on *their* nipples. Again, test drive the idea using clothespins.

Blindfolds, handcuffs, masks, and male rings:

- *Blindfolds and handcuffs:* Ah, the titillation of being blindfolded and/or handcuffed and helpless. Again, *normal* for some women; for others, it's just too threatening and scary to feel out of control. If being the helpless victim is hot for you, get a great blindfold or just use a scarf. If you experiment with handcuffs, use the Velcro® kind, not the lock and key police type. It's the *idea* of being handcuffed—the pretending—that can turn you on. So unless you know how to get out of the keyed metal handcuffs, I suggest you leave the real handcuffs for the folks on *Law and Order*. Discuss the mutual rules you set up (see Playing Doctor section) so your partner knows when to stop if the action becomes frightening for you.

- *Masks:* Do you like the idea of being the sex object that your partner coldly manipulates? If that appeals to you, then let your partner wear a mask—or both wear one. Masks give the sense of forbidden sex (see "Playing Doctor" and the fantasy discussion that follows). You can see the eyes and maybe the mouth, but you can't see the other's expression or emotion, which highly stimulates some women. In addition, it makes play fun and adds a fresh dimension with a partner of many years.

- *The Male Ring:* This is further out on the bell curve but still *normal*—that is, a ring for your man's penis. The male ring is usually a leather or fabric strap that looks like an adjustable leather watchband. It fits around the base of his penis and under his testicles so both the testicles and penis protrude above the ring. Aside from intensifying a man's erection, it can be a lifesaver for those who have an erectile challenge because it helps hold the blood in the penis during an erection. To use it, put on the male ring while the penis is soft. As your partner gets aroused, the ring keeps the blood in the penis, helping maintain his erection. After the sexual interlude, he simply unfastens the strap. Warning: You can find rings made of metal for this purpose. I suggest not using them because a real metal ring is difficult to remove in case he needs to get it off quickly. Men have actually had to go to emergency rooms to get them off. Save the sweat of worrying; use the Velcro® or leather variety instead.

❧

Highlights from Sex on the Porch
Why she loves being dominated

Leanne, 60, is a high-powered executive at a Fortune 500 company who's at the apex of her career. At **Sex on the Porch**, she confessed that she feels "tired of being in charge." When she has sex with her new partner, he is completely dominant over her. He orders her around and tells her what to do. He ties her down and "makes her comply." She loves it because it's the one time when someone else totally takes charge. When playing like this, she has no decisions to make.

Whips and ropes:

Why do people like to be whipped and/or tied up? The simple answer is this: For some people, the pain threshold of a sting or a spank from a gentle leather whip equates to sexual arousal. Being tied up suggests helpless captivity. Their hearts beat harder; they experience a brief high with it; the brain interprets that as sexual arousal and therefore so does the body. More complex responses come from enjoying being submissive to a master. For many people in high-powered leadership jobs, it's actually a relief—even a high—to have someone order them or "punish" them through whipping or tying them up (in play, of course). They're not in charge.

About buying whips and the whipping activity:

- *Purchase only soft leather made for this activity.* Don't use hard paddles or coarse material that can cut or bruise the skin. I have clients who actually "whip" using long noodles (yes, like spaghetti). Be imaginative. Start small. It's the *suggestion* that counts.

- *Aim only at the buttocks and be gentle in your motion.* Remember, this is pretend play. Don't allow the leather to touch the genitals, the breasts, or any area that houses vital organs (kidney, liver, stomach, ovaries).

- *Be careful of the "wrap around" effect.* Long whips can wrap around the body and end up with the tips landing on tender areas that shouldn't be touched. Start with small whips and very soft strokes.

- *Know your "STOP word!"* Choose a safety word that has no sexual overtones. When that word is said by either person, it means the action stops immediately. You might find an ordinary word like "worm" or "bird" works well for this purpose.

Being tied up:

If you enjoy feeling captive or submissive, this may become a favorite activity for you. Here are the rules:

- Know how to tie a slipknot that you can easily undo. This is play. When you tie up your partner, be sure he or she can easily get out of rope tie if needed.

- Buy soft rope, not clotheslines. Rope for clotheslines can be too sticky to undo and can burn when rubbing the skin. Instead, purchase gentle bungie-type cords that stretch for easy release yet can still feel tight enough to make someone feel like a prisoner. Be sure the rope's fabric is soft and pliable.

- Again, know your "STOP word!" More about "STOP words" in the role-play discussion that follows.

7. PLAYING DOCTOR

This is role-play for grown-ups—all about fantasy, dress-up (wearing a costume or other-sex clothing)—and having fun playing someone you are not.

❧

Highlights from Sex on the Porch

Mehala, 58, told us this story: "On my fourth date with him, we were ready to make love, and he walked out of the bathroom with a pair of my thong bikini panties on. I was shocked and just stood there, speechless. He coyly asked, 'Isn't this hot?' When he saw my jaw on the floor and the shock on my face, he took them off.

"Turns out his recently deceased wife loved to dress *him* up. He just assumed I would like it. But I immediately thought he might be gay. The whole mood disappeared.

"When we talked about this incident later, he apologized. It wasn't that I didn't like it; I had simply never seen it before. I didn't even know men did that! Now, a year later, we're still dating. About a month ago, I asked him to put on the panties again, just to see how I'd feel. Funny thing is, it was kind of sexy in a weird fun way. Seeing his erection inside of tiny panties is sort of cool. I have to say I love to look at it.

"Does that make me strange?"

No, Mehala isn't strange. She's *normal*. In this scene, she's playing dress-up with him. Wearing the clothing of the opposite sex can be sexy, if you are open to it. In fact, acting out the forbidden in a safe environment isn't only normal, it's healthy—assuming both partners willingly participate. However, it becomes *un*healthy and *ab*normal if one of the partners likes to dress up and keeps it a secret from his/her partner.

Of course, dress up comes in just about any form you can imagine—doctor/nurse, French maid/butler, policeman/prostitute, knight/princess, prisoner/guard. The list goes on forever. It's simply play. Not every woman includes fantasy and dress-up in her erotic adventures, of course, and that's normal for her. But if both partners want to play, watch it rev up a romantic interlude.

Fantasizing is a fabulous way to spice up intimacy. Fantasies can be private or acted out with a partner. They give us permission to think about—or pretend and play act—an action we could never live out in real life, with or without a partner. Fantasies of rape, gang bangs, doctors-gone-wrong, UPS drivers who deliver a highly personal package, exhibitionism (others are watching you have sex), voyeurism (watching other people have sex), dominance, bondage, punishment—all can be absolutely *normal* in your inner world.

The point is this: Each of us has a dark side filled with fears and desires. Through sexual fantasies and role-playing, we can address our fears of dark occurrences and make them less scary in our minds. We can also express hidden desires in safe ways. Who (except our partners if we choose to involve them) will know?

Realize that fantasies are *normal*. You own them. And you never have to share them with a partner if you elect not to.

❧

Highlights from Sex on the Porch

Tanya, 63, shared this story about fantasies: "I was watching *The Bachelor* on reality TV when my husband, at sixty years old and slightly overweight, came strolling into the family room wearing those state trooper-looking sunglasses. He wore jeans and a dark blue t-shirt that was tight. Then he said, "I'll make you talk." He grabbed my hand, pulled me up off the couch, and clasped handcuffs on me (fake ones he found at a party store). I giggled, and he shook me (okay, he "sort of" shook me). He said, 'You won't be laughing when we're finished. You're going to be begging me to stop.'

"Then he took my clothes off me, one piece at a time, and ordered me to lie down on the coach. After that, well, whew—we went through it all. He ordered me to do stuff to him and even to myself while he watched. What fun!

"Problem was that the phone rang at the very end, just as we were getting to the climax (no pun). We both laughed, knowing it would be our son Ted. That phone call killed the energy, but we sure had fun until then. We never could have done this when the kids lived at home. Never.

"I love it when he plays the bad cop. It really turns me on."

Fantasy can take place on a variety of levels. It might just be a scene in your mind that you envision as you pleasure yourself or during a great sexual interlude with a partner (or a not-so-great one so you let your fantasy take you out of the boredom!).

For women who are single or in a sex-flat partnership (for whatever reason: boredom, routine, illness), our imagination can be a life saver. Remember, our brains recognize fantasy as being close to reality, so escaping into a titillating landscape can be a blessing for many women—as good as or even better than the real thing. Fortunately as women, most of us are hard-wired to run a complete story in our minds. So when we take that creative visualization into our bedrooms, our sexual selves come alive.

Most men aren't as fortunate. Their hard wiring makes them highly visual and they operate in the moment. Imagining a fantasy setting in a man's mind might contribute to his arousal, but he needs it to be backed up with something to *look at*—a woman's body next to him, an erotic DVD, a magazine. By comparison, most women are blessed to be turned on by both real-life and imagined happenings.

Now, some men who understand a women's ability to play out a complete fantasy in her head want her to share the story playing in her head as the arousal gets intense. The turn on for him is *seeing* her getting aroused by the fantasy. He might get a little hotter listening to her story. Pleasure, not performance, kicks in.

Men generally love hearing what women think, particularly if the man is included in the story. It can be hot and fun to tell "bedtime stories" of made-up sexual fantasies, but it's not easy for every woman to describe her fantasy out loud, especially during sex. Guilt, embarrassment, and perfectionism can enter into the equation. Yet when we learn to let go of those, storytelling can be titillating. Still, if feelings of discomfort or awkwardness get in the way, you can save telling him the story for later.

❦

Titillating Tip
How to create erotic role-playing

- *Suggest the role-play to your partner first.* Discuss your role-playing fantasy with your partner before you begin. Don't simply say, "Let's play doctor." Instead, start with, "I thought this might be fun. What if we pretend to be doctor and nurse (or whatever scene you prefer)? What do you think?" Give your partner a chance to respond. Let him or her get used to the idea.

- *Set expectations and boundaries.* Talking about a fantasy can be titillating, but that's not the point of discussing it before you do it. You want to protect yourself from letting events get away from you. If you like the idea of his wearing your panties or having him dress up as a cop or having *you* dominate him (or any other activity that feels out of your comfort zone), talk about specifics first. You can set boundaries together by agreeing on a "STOP word."

- *Create a "STOP word."* When either of you says the "STOP word," all play stops immediately because something is wrong. However, do NOT select the actual word "stop" as your word. Why? Because partners may play scenes that involve dominance of one over another, and part of the play is begging the other to stop. If you say "stop" in this context, your partner will think you're still acting. So choose a short word you both can remember. (*Tip:* Words like "existential" don't work!) Pick a name you both know that won't come up as part of the role-play. For me, that might be "Dot," my mother's name. (I know her moniker won't come up as part of the role-play, and I definitely won't forget it.) Or select a common word like "worm." Keep it simple, easy to remember, and categorically not sexy!

8. **FETISHES: food, leather, balloons, and more**

For some, it's titillating to touch or be touched by an actual object. If you like to have feathers in your bed when you are making love, that's normal for you. Again, as long as no one is hurt physically or psychologically, I consider almost anything okay.

Frequently, leather, soft plastic, shoes, and whips are associated with fetishes. In fact, if you can imagine an object——balloons, noodles, fruit, ponies, panties, hats, sunglasses—it's likely a fetish to someone. Let me be clear: *Having a fetish doesn't mean you want to have sex with the object. It means having that object close by turns you on.*

Leather clothing is, perhaps, the most common fetish. Shoes, vests, skirts, jackets, pants (some without crotches!), panties, bras, you name it. Out there further on the bell curve is the body harness, with its leather straps circling the body to make it look like a 21st Century Spartacus.

For some couples, wearing a body harness turns them on, which is *normal* for them. (*Tip:* If this floats your boat but have no idea where or how to get a body harness, contact me at info@getasecondwind.com. I will direct you to one of many stores that can get you set up with a leather harness.)

❧

Highlights from Sex on the Porch

Rebecca, 59, got turned on by literally winding her partner up in a giant knot of yard. She started at his head and wound the yarn around him, leaving his face open. She gave him plenty of use of arms and legs while leaving his genitals alone. Along the way, she kissed him and laid on him, rubbing her nude body against his yarn-covered corpus. When she finished, they made love—with him still wrapped up in yarn. Although it never really turned *him* on, she loved it. And he got excited just watching her.

9. VOYEURISM/EXHIBITIONISM: love to watch

These two sides of the same coin can be part of your sex play. Indeed, the billion-dollar pornography / erotica industry is all about voyeurism—that is, watching other people have sex.

❧

Titillating Tip
A word about pornography/erotica

Is it normal to watch erotica with a partner? Yes and yes. For seasoned women, the golden rule for watching any type of adult movie is this: *Do not compare yourself or your partner to the actors on the screen.* They are actors who auditioned for their breast size, erection length, and body appeal! They retake the scene if someone gets a foot cramp or forgets a line. They might even stop in the middle of a hot scene for a lunch break. But just like the rest of us, they walk off the set at the end of a shoot, get in their cars, drive to the grocery store, and buy milk and cat food.

It's a job, folks. The male actors take Viagra® so they can stay erect all day. Minutes before they're filmed panting and begging and sucking, they were sipping a latte and talking with the director and camera operators about the right angle for the scene. So don't compare your sexual encounters with theirs! Just relax and enjoy the titillation that they present to you, letting it arouse you.

Because men tend to be more visual than women, most erotica/pornography is created for men. Here's my unresearched explanation: In primitive times, for survival, men had to quickly get aroused and impregnate their female mates. That's why Mother Nature gave men a cleared pathway from the eyes to the penis. The age-old porn industry has been built on that premise.

As a seasoned woman, you can make erotica work well for you, too. However, don't expect hotel room porn to excite you. One **Sex on the Porch** attendee told us about turning on hotel erotica during a romantic getaway. She said, "The actor nailed the actress sexually in the first five minutes, and it was a giant *yawn* after that."

It's easy to see that porn in hotel rooms is intended for men to masturbate to ejaculation within the first five minutes. After that, the action slows down. Chances are most men fall asleep right after ejaculating! (*Tip:* If you're on a romantic interlude, *bring your own erotica.* Don't count on the hotel movie system to heat you up. Check out my website at www.getasecondwind.com and click on Products for wonderful erotica for women. Your man will enjoy it, too.)

If you are single, erotica is a wonderful way to enjoy flying solo. Close the drapes, get comfy, and enjoy yourself—literally. Let the fantasy carry you away.

- *Exhibitionism and the seasoned woman:* As women, we're skirting exhibitionism when we wear low-cut dresses, garters and boa-bordered nighties, or tight outfits of any kind. We love the reaction we get. In the bedroom, subtle or blatant, it's part of what we do. Stripping for your partner, you become the exhibitionist and your partner the voyeur. Remember, most men get turned on visually. He loves to look at you, so take advantage of that! Remember, they say the perfect body is not what gets them going; it's the attitude she projects that they like. (For more on this topic, see Part IV.)

- *A note about men:* Many men enjoy having you look at them naked, especially when they are aroused. Let's be honest here. A man considers his penis to be his pride and joy, and that doesn't change in his lifetime. He loves to be an exhibitionist parading it in front of you—a real turn on for him. Indeed, looking and commenting on it often leads to great ends, if you feel comfortable doing so. Especially at midlife-plus when a full erection may prove difficult, allowing him to "show off" boosts his ego. Before you decide that's not what you want to do, remember that, for him, it's no different than his telling you how beautiful you look. It makes you feel wonderful. That's how your man will feel.

Highlights from Sex on the Porch

At one session, Marguerite told me privately what she and her boyfriend love to do. She'd ask her boyfriend to sit on the deck outside her bedroom and watch her as she came in to the room (as if coming from work). She'd strip in front of the glass door while he watched from the outside. Then she'd lie down on the bed and play with herself in full view of his eyes. He'd watch and, when she'd worked herself up to high arousal, he'd burst into the room as if to take advantage of her. Together, they'd continue the adventure. At times, he'd even use gentle handcuffs on her, making the pretend captive *super* hot.

ACTIVITIES 10 – 13

Not to Be Left Out!

Dozens more activities could be named, but here are four more for your pleasuring menu selection:

10. BDSM: Bondage, Discipline, Sado-Masochistic

In Bondage, Discipline, Sado-Masochistic, often referred to as "kink," one person likes to be in charge and order the other to do whatever he/she pleases. The dominant person is often called the "top" or "dom;" the submissive person is the "bottom" or "sub." This is *normal* (and quite desirable) for some people because it can add a new dimension when "kink" is *gently* used to expand the bedroom repertoire. Bondage, of course, uses ropes, blindfolds, any type of restraint. Discipline refers to the ordering around, whipping, and spanking mentioned earlier. Sado-Masochistic or SM comes from the Marquis de Sade in France who enjoyed inflicting torture on others as part of his sexual arousal.

In playful, *non-hurtful* terms, SM means enjoying the spanking or gentle whipping. The masochism part means enjoying the *pain* inflicted upon yourself by spanking or whipping. They go well together! When you set up a natural, caring scenario, no one gets hurt physically or psychologically. It's just a way to participate in forbidden acts in a safe environment and have fun. Needless to say, agreeing to a "STOP word" is imperative for this type of play.

11. CELIBACY: the choice to abstain

Yes, it's okay to be celibate! If you have decided you would rather not express yourself sexually through physical sexual activities, that's a perfectly fine option. As with any other choice, *it must come from a positive place of love for yourself.* The same criteria apply here as with other activities: It's *normal* if it doesn't hurt you or anyone else, physically or psychologically.

If celibacy is your choice, check it against your reasoning—that is, don't regard it as punishment to yourself or another, and never do it out of self-loathing.

Think of it this way: Your body is a beautiful creation. It may not act or look the way you ideally want it to look, but it's the body you have. The pure pleasure aspect of sex, whether by yourself or with another, is a blessing that comes with your body—whether you choose to use it for pleasure or not. Again, you can make celibacy a good selection if you choose it out of love for yourself.

Plus, don't feel locked into that choice for a lifetime. I have met dozens of men and women who have stated *unequivocally* that their sex lives are Over. Forever. Why do they make that declaration? There are as many reasons as there are dating services (lots!): partner died, partner cheated, emotional pain was too much, haven't had a partner in years and don't want one now or later. Then, miraculously, amazingly, the love of their life appears, and they're celibate no more. I get a kick out of the sheepish grins and hearing "oh well" and the "never say never."

Truth is, you never stop being that sexual person you were born to be. This means finding ways you can express your sexuality other than through physical sex—like just being close with another person, even a friend, and letting music and dance light up to our sexual side. Because touch is critical to one's survival, be sure to get "touch" in other ways: a massage, a manicure, a pedicure, big hugs and back rubs from family and friends. Just don't go without!

12. BODY CHANGES: low libido (sex drive)

In the second half of life, having a low sex drive isn't unusual for many women. It appears for a variety of reasons such as:

- *Situational:* Life situations such as stressful events or illnesses can demand your attention. Don't worry. It's normal for your libido to return when the stress lifts.

- *No interest in sex from a partner:* If you feel your sex drive is low because of no interest from your partner, it's time to re-energize the relationship. Start with the communication skills discussed in Chapter 8, page 117, to open the conversation. Seeing a counselor is also an option. Please contact me if you would like help to revive your mutual passion at info@getasecondwind.com.

- *As the estrogen fades, so does the libido.* Low estrogen leading to low sex drive creates little need for physical sex. However, that doesn't mean you don't need to be touched and loved. Be sure to get those *sensual* needs met. If your estrogen level is low and you feel okay with it, it means you're probably expressing your uniqueness as a woman in other ways—your work or avocation, a sport you love, the way you dress, getting intimacy from being a good friend, mother, grandmother, or aunt. (*Tip:* If you get into a relationship and you'd like to be physically sexual again, talk to your doctor about testosterone treatment or hormone replacement therapy [HRT]. Testosterone, the hormone of desire, can give your sex drive a big boost … but it must be prescribed by a medical professional.)

Two distinct schools of thought exist about estrogen replacement or HRT. Some professionals believe HRT increases the chances of breast or uterine cancer; other professionals say its benefits—stronger bones, vaginal lubrication, regulated mood swings—offset the risks. Some professionals advocate bio-identical hormones that supposedly mimic your natural hormone equation. Learn about this option, especially as it relates to your own family history, then decide if it's right for you. It's your call.

Be careful about "natural" over-the-counter supplements that promise estrogen replacement. Many have not gone through thorough research protocols. Instead, get a "natural" prescription from a naturopathic doctor, Chinese medicine practitioner, or nutritionist, but not over the Internet (unless it's from the website of a practitioner you know and trust).

SSRIs and SSNIs are antidepressants like Prozac, Pacil, Effixor, etc., that can affect one's libido. Sometimes changing medications helps, but in general, these kinds of meds tend to lower libido energy. Diabetes, heart meds, pain meds, and cancer treatments can affect it, too. Although illness and/or medication often reduce one's sex drive, most meds can be adjusted to minimize that outcome. Expect your libido to be right there for you when you stop taking the drug. (*Tip:* Always tell your doctor if you feel sexually "down" after taking any medications. Adjustments can be made.)

If you're taking drugs for the long term and they interfere with your love life, ask your doctor for help. Don't give up. You can also call me for a referral to a sexuality specialist who helps you fit a new intimate routine into your life while you still take the necessary medications. Never give up on getting your sexuality needs met!

13. ENHANCERS: food, drugs, and other aphrodisiacs to enhance lovemaking

Food as aphrodisiac! Yes, really. As long as civilization has been around, women and men have ingested multiple things to make them amorous. It's still true today; if a substance enhances the sexual experience, people take it. Is it normal to use this stuff? It's just fine if it doesn't hurt you (or another person) physically or psychologically. Certainly, none of the foods listed here will hurt you (unless you have allergies, of course).

What's in the basic sex food group? Chocolate, oysters, and honey, of course.

- *Chocolate (yes, really).* It's at the top of the aphrodisiac list for good reason. First, it contains *phenylethamine*. Sounds like a petroleum product for your car, doesn't it? Believe me, it's not. It triggers endorphins, those heavenly compounds associated with pleasure. Even more appealing, it's loaded with antioxidants, which cause maximum blood flow. Combine all that with feeling sexy, getting aroused, and bingo! You've got fun and excitement—not to mention unfettered blood flow to parts of the body where engorgement increases sensitivity and erotic adventures.

- *Oysters.* Yep, these famous love enhancers can really do the trick. They drip with *dopamine*, the compound that stirs feelings of desire and pleasure. Dopamine can make you dopey in the best way possible. And listen to this: Oysters also encourage production of testosterone, the hormone of desire. Ladies, testosterone is not just for men anymore.

- *Honey.* Yes, really! Centuries ago, newlyweds in Europe drank honey for a month to improve their sexual stamina so they would produce a child sooner rather than later—hence the word "honeymoon." This custom reflected interest in the stamina of *both* the husband and the wife. It works because honey—the pure organic kind, not processed honey—has a reasonable number of antioxidants. Remember, antioxidants help reduce inflammation in blood vessels and provide maximum blood flow to those essential erotically charged organs.

～∽⌒∽～

Titillating Tip

Turn chocolate tasting into an erotic adventure.

The number one rule is, of course, have fun. And here are three steps to get you primed:

- *Buy the best chocolate you can find.* The percentage of cocoa has to be at least 70%. The higher the percentage, the higher the antioxidants, and the more likely you are to feel the aphrodisiac qualities of the chocolate. Buy two different brands of chocolate for comparison.

- *Set the stage.* Keep in mind that you don't have to be "in the mood" to taste chocolate. Starting the process will awaken that mood. Turn down the music, get soft light (you must be able to see each other as well as the chocolate), and find some place cozy to sit next to each other. Wear comfortable clothes (or nothing at all) and make sure you've washed off any perfumes or colognes. Lay out the chocolate and a palate cleanser (such as slices of apple or sourdough bread) on a beautiful tray. Uncork your favorite wine and set out wine glasses (or a pitcher of water if you don't drink wine). Turn off your cell phones and house phone ringer.

- *Take your time.* One of the joys after 50, 60, 70 years is knowing that it's truly the journey, not the destination—especially when it comes to erotic chocolate tasting. Use all five senses. See the chocolate, smell it, taste it, touch it, hear it snap. Along the way, you'll find yourself using all five senses with your partner, too. Now that you're ready to start, here's a step-by-step guide to chocolate tasting for lovers:

  1. Be still. Close your eyes and take three deep breaths. Give your partner a long, warm kiss.

  2. Open the chocolate bars. LOOK at them. The color should be glossy. Notice the imprint or insignia the chocolatier has made on the chocolate.

3. Break off a piece and LISTEN to the "snap." The higher the cocoa content, the louder the snap. Indeed, professionals judge its quality by the sound of the snap. Give your partner another long kiss to celebrate the snap.

4. TOUCH the piece and rub it a bit. Fingers will do but c'mon … Go ahead and use any part of your body except your mouth. Did you know that chocolate melts at 97 degrees F? How convenient! The warmth of your body will melt the chocolate and release its odors. It should feel smooth and even. You can lick it off each other if this gets messy…

5. After the aroma has been released from light rubbing, offer a piece to your partner to SMELL. When you first start smelling chocolate, you may not get the subtleties. Don't give up. You'll soon be able to smell an incredible array of scents.

6. Place a square in your own mouth and then your partner's. Let it begin to melt. TASTE the flavors and FEEL the sensation on your tongue. You can chew it, but only three times. What new flavors are released? Try each sample, one at a time, and check out the differences.

7. Notice the finish. Like good wine, the finish—the lingering taste—counts for a lot. Is it bitter or unpleasant? What do you

taste after the chocolate is swallowed? Do you want more? Go for it!

8. Pour yourself a glass of wine and have your way with the rest of the chocolate—and your lover—as you please. Turn up the music, turn down the lights, kiss your partner one more time, and work chocolate into the equation somehow. Let the creative juices flow!

Note on wine: If you'd like to pair the wine and chocolate, keep in mind that the greater the percentage of cocoa, the deeper and richer the wine should be. I suggest you pair your 60% chocolate with a Pinot Noir. Select a Shiraz, with its fruit-and-vanilla edge to accompany your 70% chocolate. The bold 80%+ chocolate calls for the cinnamon and berry flavor of Zinfandel.

- *Drugs to "get it on."* What about Viagra® (Sildenafil), Cialis® (Tadalafil) and Levitra® (Vardenafil), the mighty triumvirate of erections? Is there really better living through chemistry? Are most men taking a little blue pill at midlife and beyond? Is it *normal*?

It's certainly normal for men to want the erections of a 25 year old. Many men over 55 choose not to use these drugs, however. At the risk of oversimplifying, the drugs just aren't as powerful as they were once believed to be. Yes, some men in the second half of life have found success with Viagra® et al; they're delighted to use them. However, many experience the side effects—headache, congestion, sneezing, coughing, racing heart, dizziness to name just a few—and say they aren't worth the potential erection. Besides, men taking medications for heart disease can't take them; men taking HIV drugs can't come near them.

In addition, a man can develop a psychological dependency on the drug, convincing himself he can't "get it up" without it. Whether he can or can't becomes a moot point. If he's in China on his honeymoon and his Viagra® is back in San Francisco, chances are he won't get an erection—not because he can't but because he *thinks* he can't.

The biggest reason men stop taking the wonder drug of erections, though, is that intimacy and connection have nothing to do with drugs. If you have trouble connecting with your partner or need to find your way out of a flat sex life, drugs won't make it happen. You need help with your communication, not the firmness of his penis.

⤫

Red Flag!

Use caution when buying over-the-counter drugs for your man's erectile dysfunction!

A note about dealing with erectile dysfunction with untested drugs from the Internet or adult stores: If they sound too good to be true, they are! Some are harmless, but some are outright dangerous.

For example, one capsule sold in adult stores is called *Stiff Nights*. No kidding. Lack of creative naming notwithstanding, this drug is intended for just that—stiff nights. Does it work because the guy thinks it will? I know a guy in his mid 60s who uses herbal aids regularly and swears by them. Does he get an erection because something in the drug actually stimulated his central nervous system? No one knows because it's never been officially tested and regulated. I'm not saying never take drugs like this; I'm saying be careful. Caveat emptor.

- *Fruit of the vine (wine or any alcohol).* Is drinking alcohol a help or hindrance to physical intimacy?

As a seasoned woman (and for men, too), orgasm and arousal become more difficult as more alcohol enters the body. It also dehydrates the system, making lubrication even more difficult. Therefore, if you want to drink and have sex, you'd better "get it on" in the first 30 minutes. (*Tip:* In the second half of life, you can stop racing through sex. If you take the emphasis *off* intercourse and focus on pleasure, not performance, then alcohol is not needed.)

❧

Highlights from Sex on the Porch

Suzanne, 67, asked me if it's normal to have a glass of wine before sex. It seems that several fellows she has dated have insisted that sex is better with a drink beforehand. I suspect that the alcohol is more about relaxing than good sex. In fact, I know that's true. Alcohol, a depressant, plays a little trick on us at the beginning of tasting. I call it The Chianti Effect.

> What is it? For about the first 30 minutes after your first sip, you feel euphoria setting in. You're friendly with everyone, more confident, more assertive than before. Then the depressant aspect of alcohol kicks in and you spend the rest of the evening trying to get The Chianti Effect back. That 30 minutes may just provide the jumpstart that you need to get going sexually, but don't depend on it for the rest of the encounter.

- *Mary Jane and friends.* What about marijuana and sex? You'll hear people extol the virtues of sex and pot, bragging about long orgasms, extra sensitive skin. But does all that really happen? For some people, yes, and for others, no. Try it for yourself when you're not under pressure. Like any drug, marijuana reacts uniquely in each person. Is it *normal* to use marijuana during sex? Yes, if you both enjoy using it. No, if either of you feels uncomfortable about it.

  From where I sit, there's a significant placebo effect with pot—that is, if you think it's working, it is. Marijuana makes some women feel hot and sexy and gives some men an erection, but just as many others want to go to sleep. It's unpredictable. And with any drug, too much will ruin just about any romantic interlude.

- *Poppers and sniffers.* What about over-the-counter enhancers like Poppers? Poppers are little eyedropper-sized bottles of a glue-like substance that, when sniffed, makes you feel high. Your heart races and the blood flows.

  Poppers and the other sexual intensifiers are sold in adult toy stores (sex shops). Because many of them are controversial, you might have to ask a clerk for them. Is taking them *normal*? By our definition of not hurting you psychologically or physically, the jury is out concerning safety and effectiveness. Because they aren't regulated, we can't be sure if they're safe. And they can be very dangerous if taken in excess or in combination with other drugs.

Is it *normal* to take these? If you are a risk taker, yes. If you want assurance they are safe, no. My advice? Steer away from them. Go back to chocolate. Arousal might take a little longer, but it's a lot safer! (*Tip:* As a seasoned woman, be wise enough not to be foolish. Take care when experimenting with Poppers.)

Highlights from Sex on the Porch

At one gathering, Molly, 56, enlightened us about her encounter with Poppers. She and her boyfriend Sam, 59, sniffed them—supposedly good for erections and feeling empowered. (They're found at shady sex shops, never on my website!). She was feeling sexy and strong. They began to have intercourse on the bed and, with all the fervor of the crazed moment, she slid to the side of the bed, her head hanging off the edge. As he pounded her, she arched to make the position better and POP, her back gave out.

That night, she knew something had happened, later learning that she'd cracked a rib! The next morning, she could hardly move. The boyfriend had gone, but she had a lasting memory of their evening together that gave new meaning to the word Poppers. She said she'll never use these over-the-counter enhancers again.

CHECKLIST TIME

New possibilities abound for you as a seasoned woman. Take a moment and identify what you would like to add, subtract, or investigate in your physical sexuality. After all, you're a woman of action. Own it!

ACTIVITY	I like it	I want to try it	I don't like it	Talk to partner
1. Intercourse: - use more lubrication - use a condom - new positions - find alternatives to intercourse				
2. Kissing				
3. Touch: - holding hands - massage - tickling/pinching - hand jobs - spanking - masturbation				
4. Oral Sex				

ACTIVITY	I like it	I want to try it	I don't like it	Talk to partner
5. Anal Sex				
6. Masturbation				

7. Sex Toys:
  - vibrators
  - dildos
  - nipple clamps
  - others I'm interested in				

8. Playing Doctor: - role-playing for grown ups				

9. Fetishes:
  - food
  - leather
  - balloons
  - others I'm interested in				

10. Voyeur Exhibitionist:
  - love to watch
  - love to be watched				

11. Celibacy				
12. Body Changes: - low libido				

ACTIVITY	I like it	I want to try it	I don't like it	Talk to partner
13.Enhancers:				
- aphrodisiac foods				
• chocolate				
• oysters				
• honey				
- Viagra®, Cialis®, Levitra®				
- alcohol				
- marijuana				
- over-the-counter enhancers like poppers				

CHAPTER 6

What's Not Normal, Ever?

Anything that causes physical or psychological harm to anyone, including you, is not normal—ever.

We're talking about the underbelly of sexuality—the dark side. No doubt you've seen the exploitation of this delicate subject with ugly pornography, rape, abuse, and so on. Using sex for power, withholding sex, being unfaithful, "going on the down low" (meaning married straight men seeking anonymous sex with other men) are more examples.

The list goes on and on.

❦

Red Flag!
Beware!

Here are the parameters of what's NOT normal:

- Inappropriate sexual "acting out" (aggressive verbal or physical behavior that makes you feel uncomfortable)
- Physical abuse (pain inflicted without consent)
- Not stopping when the "STOP word" is given
- Coercion or involuntary participation

- Confusion about who your sex partner is (drugs are often used to inhibit cognitive recognition)
- Inability to ascertain risks (due to drugs or bullying)
- Inability to say no (due to drugs or bullying)
- Inability to state what level of intimacy is okay
- Self pleasuring or exposure in public
- Activities not consistent with beliefs and values
- Abusing drugs for pleasure
- Addiction to sex: When the driving need to have sex interferes with the normal daily living routine; sex is sought out in spite of having to take great risks for yourself and/or for those around you.

If you find yourself involved in any of these situations, it's time to get help. Do it immediately.

Start by telling a trusted friend what's happening. Then ask that friend to "hold your hand" while you get professional help. (If you're physically in harm's way, call 911 immediately.)

If you believe your immediate safety is threatened, call the police or 911 on the spot. Better to have officers come and find you safe than wait until the activities spiral out of your control.

Remember, sex is intended to be pleasurable, not a life-threatening nightmare. Get help ASAP.

❧

ALWAYS KNOW THIS:

You have the right to stop any sexual activity at any time, with no explanation. If you are uncomfortable, that is reason in itself. An *appropriate* partner will always understand.

Sexual Mistreatment

In my experience, most women have experienced some form of sexual mistreatment in their lives. From being surprised by an exhibitionist to actual rape or vaginal penetration from an inappropriate person, most women have faced a sexual violation at some time.

Recognize that you can experience wrongful intrusion at many levels. Getting past your toughest memories might require a lifetime of hard work. Frequently, young women who encountered minor experiences have come to terms with it by midlife and successfully let them go. For those who faced severe, malicious abuse, though, their memories might be a huge roadblock to experiencing sexual happiness.

Your body is a beautiful masterpiece, your sexuality a work of art. At midlife and beyond, it's imperative that you work with a professional to reframe and redefine the meaning of any atrocities you might have experienced so you can enjoy healthy sexuality on your terms without trauma. If your childhood experiences haunt you today, don't delay. See a psychologist specializing in sexual abuse. Consider it money well spent. (If you don't know where to turn, contact me at info@getasecondwind.com. I will help find the right professional for you.)

Highlights from Sex on the Porch

I could tell Leslie was nervous. As we talked about role-playing in sexual trysts, she looked like she wanted to cry. When I asked if she were okay, she said, "Is it normal to play doctor, in the altogether, with a girlfriend?" It's something she had done when she was eight years old. I asked if they had both willingly participated and she chortled, "Yes, over and over again. Is that wrong?"

In fact, it's very right! Many children make out with each other, play with each other's genitals, even have rudimentary intercourse and oral sex before they get to puberty. The only people who make it wrong are the adults who project their own sexual insecurities onto the situation. Consider what happens in nature: Young mammals have sexual play with each other as part of growing up.

In my counseling, grown men and women reveal that they still carry guilt about playing doctor with a friend and exploring genitalia well before puberty. If that's you, rest assured it's normal to play doctor (or other exploratory play) either with a same-sex friend or a friend of the opposite sex. You're following your natural curiosity and responding to newfound sensations that feel good. It's part of learning about your sexuality—a journey that goes on from birth to death.

However, if you were coerced into the play or forced against your will, that's a different discussion.

Professional help may be needed to help you realize you didn't ask for it, deserve it, or did something wrong that led to it. Abuse of power is what you experienced.

Most children get exploited in some way or another sexually, sometimes in a very minor way (e.g., your older friend invites you to watch porn and you are too embarrassed to say no). Sometimes it's in the form of exhibitionism. It could even be full-blown sexual abuse from an inappropriate, dysfunctional adult.

In your second half of life, you can let go of those memories. Again, get professional help if these scenarios are getting in the way of relaxing with your sexuality. Find a licensed professional who specializes in sexual abuse. No one with those memories should have to suffer. (Again, if you don't know anyone, contact me at info@getasecondwind.com and I will help you find one that's right for you.)

Part Three

THE DATING GAME—
STARTING OVER

*"When we talk so openly [at Sex on the Porch] about getting back
into the dating game, I'm tapping into feelings of anticipation and
excitement that I haven't felt in years. I feel like an awkward teenager
all over again. And I was the head of HR in a huge corporation!"*
~ Diane, 68, **Sex on the Porch** participant

The good news and the "challenging" news: This generation of 55+ women is more youthful, more vital, more ageless, healthier, wealthier, better medicated, and more energized than any generation of women preceding us. That's the good news. That means, on average, we'll live a longer life than those in previous generations and enjoy a host of new possibilities: second and third occupations, new relationships, opportunities for splendid sex, and a whole new phenomenon: Dating. Yes, the fastest growing group in online dating is the over-50 crowd!

These days, we're living long enough to start over. It's possible serial relationships might become the wave of the future—that is, having the right relationship at the right time, and then moving on. Here's the "challenging news." This wave requires you to learn what might be a completely new skill: *how to date.*

CHAPTER 7

Dating and Sexual Dilemmas for Women Ages 55, 65, 75

Ah, dating. Decades ago, who ever thought we'd be dating in our mid 50s, 60s, 70s, and beyond!? Yet, here we are. Charles Dickens famously wrote in *A Tale of Two Cities* this phrase that rings true today: "It was the best of times and the worst of times."

Truth told, dating can be hilariously joyful at one time and overwhelmingly terrifying at another. One minute your ego is flattered by the attention you're getting; the next minute you're dealing with rejection. Remember, like everything else in life, dating is a process. If you hang in there, it can be lots of fun. It can even be highly rewarding when you find a new partner—someone who's just right for you.

However, to find your new partner, you must first *believe* that you will, and then you have to make a plan. Your plan starts with a list of the qualities you want in that person. Keep your list in your purse and look at it frequently. If you do this, you'll attract the partner of your dreams! Still, if you feel bogged down with the process, don't let it get to you. Stop if it feels overwhelming, knowing you can pick it up again whenever you want.

The good news? Successful dating and partnering over 55 *can and does* happen for both sexes—not just for the post-graduate equivalent of the cutsie cheerleader and the cool football captain.

How do you get connected? Of course, there's the traditional trio of friend fix-ups, going to bars, and joining interest groups. These days, though, the over-55 daters jump on the Internet—and they aren't only signing on to the well-known dating match-up sites such as eHarmony, Match.com, or JDate. Some online services are devoted to "seniors" or "mature adults"—that is, midlife-plus daters. (*Tip:* Do an online search for "senior dating" and a whole host of sites will present themselves.)

The need for good relationships that can lead to good sex continues throughout the lifespan. Many centurions (people over 100 years old) are still having sex! Besides, for the 55+ crowd, dating availability increases with age because of spouses dying or divorcing.

❧

Titillating Tips
The right mix …

With the right attitude and these ingredients, midlife-plus dating can be a winning proposition. Consider these 13 dating tips:

1. Keep your sense of humor. Have fun. What else it there? Don't take yourself too seriously.

2. Remember that all three legs of the stool—financial, psychological, physical—count in a solid relationship. If your prospective new partner scores high on each of these legs, you might have a winner.

3. Move on to someone else if the time spent with the person you're dating simply doesn't feel right. It probably doesn't feel right to her/him, either.

Don't waste precious time. And don't settle for second best! Your mother said it: There are other fish in the sea.

4. Carry condoms with you. This generation tends to rebel against using condoms, mostly because of being in long-term relationships and skipping over the AIDS epidemic. Today, the threat of getting infected is alive and well.

5. Learn to ask if your new sex partner is *clean*, meaning clear of any STIs (sexually transmitted infections). Most women shy away from asking because they feel embarrassed. But get real; those in the 55+ population have one of the fastest growing HIV diagnosis rates.

6. Carry lubricant. Because women's vaginas are drier after menopause, using lots of lube makes intercourse possible—and pleasurable.

7. Request intimacy over intercourse. In bed, take the emphasis off intercourse and let go of the orgasm-mania you felt in your 20s and 30s. Think *pleasure*, not performance.

8. Ladies—men are worried about performance. Be understanding and patient.

9. Men—ladies are worried about body image. Be complimentary with your dates.

10. Make a habit of telling your friends where you are going with your date, even when you've been fixed up with a friend of a friend. Check in by calling a buddy half way through the date, *especially* if

you met your date online. Consider this a non-negotiable security precaution.

11. Meet your date for the first time in a neutral, central place like a coffee house or an open restaurant.

12. Never get in a car with your date the first time you see each other. Meet him/her at a public destination, driving yourself there and home. Maintain your independence and you'll stay safe.

13. Always reserve time to spend with your lifelong girlfriends. They will sustain your spirits long after your latest love-interest has gone away.

Sex and the Uniqueness of Midlife-Plus for Dating Singles

By midlife, you've had a myriad of adventures and developed a lot of habits. How you habitually express your sexuality becomes a habit, too. When you stay with one partner for many years, it's likely you have a certain routine. It's likely you'll take that routine into your new relationships. Similarly, your new partner will bring in his old familiar patterns.

Yet, his habits and yours won't match at all, I guarantee. What was *normal* for you may not be normal for him, and vice versa. It's time for being open, accepting, and non-judgmental. Don't take what he does personally. Like you, he's doing the best he can with what he has learned. Always avoid labeling him as "wrong." Instead, expect surprises and create new sexual routines that are uniquely adventurous to both of you.

In that vein, when he does something that's strange for you, take the Zen route and think, "That's an interesting way of doing that." Don't assume he's too aggressive or too subtle. Just know he's doing what he's learned to do over the years. Remember, he has no idea what your preferences are. Communication is key. After your initial intimate interludes, open the conversation about your experiences. Tell him what you liked and what you would rather sidestep. Ask him what he liked and what changes he'd like you to make. If you have to postpone the conversation, find a time to talk about it at the first opportunity. It's critical to building an ongoing connection.

Yes, I know. As young girls, you were taught to "follow your dance partner." While that may have been the right move then, doing so today could prevent developing honest intimacy and enjoyment with your current partner. Times have changed. Take the initiative and talk!

～◦～

Highlights from Sex on the Porch

Kathy, 66, told us how she kept her sense of humor on her fourth date with Glen, 69. She had checked her make-up and decided she looked younger without her glasses, so off they came. She's ready to flirt. As they had previously decided, tonight would be their first real intimate occasion. Where's the lube? She grabbed the sample in the foil packet, then went off to Glen's. Hours later, sheets move, hands wander, mouths connect, breath comes fast. Kathy grabs the lube, rips open the packet, and lowers it under the sheets. Suddenly Glen stops fondling her. What's that smell? Nail polish remover! Oops. Wrong foil product! Kathy's note to self: Keep glasses on when locating lube!

Today, after five years of marriage, Kathy and Glen are still together and still laughing about the caustic lube. The lesson? Laugh at the foibles and don't trust faulty vision!

⌒⌒

Kat's Quip
Meeting the Right Man

Do you want to meet an interesting man? Have you been a success in your life and you want to engage with a guy of equal success?

1. Start telling yourself you *will* meet him. Every day, three times a day, repeat it. I mean it. Your brain needs to know you are serious, and this meeting is top priority to you.

2. Stop spending your spare time—or your whole life—going to garden clubs, newcomers groups, or coffee klatches with other women. Do you see any potential partners there? No. It's time to open up energy and space for your new man. And quit telling everyone around you there are no men available!

3. Put away any baggy clothes and start showing your body with pride! For men, it's all about the attitude, not the size. Remember, they're highly visual.

Put on your big-girl sexy panties and put yourself out there where he can find you.

CHAPTER 8

How to Say What You
Need to Say about Sex

In my counseling sessions, women clients have said, "Why won't he do that the *normal* way?" or "How can he expect me to do it *that way*?" Well, he does it *that way* because it's what feels *normal* for him. Bingo! This sparks the right moment for a good conversation with the partner. Because each person sees things differently, a meeting of the minds is needed to establish what's normal for your relationship.

If you have a partner and you communicate well, *normal for you* means you both agree doing something is fun. Alternatively, you're willing to try that something out of curiosity *with complete trust in your partner.* That means if you're dating in a committed way and your partner springs a zinger on you (such as bringing out a butt plug), you would participate only after talking about it. Remember, it's *not* normal to be forced against your will.

In fact, when people *don't* talk about doing something sexually, things like this happen: After a painful divorce, you decide that you are *done* with slamming your head into the headboard in "doggie style" intercourse that your former husband craved. No more bracing yourself while he bangs away! You can give up on this position completely, or you can talk to your new partner about it. Voice your concerns. He might help you enjoy the position from a new gentle perspective. Or you might find that he secretly doesn't like it, either. You'll never know unless you ask! A whole new world could open up to you. But you have to take the first step and talk about it.

By the way, most men will not instigate a conversation about sexual activities. Don't wait for him to read your mind (guess what—he won't anyway). Put yourself out there and talk about it. Make this an investment in *you*.

~~~

Titillating Tips
Talk about it!

Being sexual with a partner can be a set-up for misunderstanding for these three reasons:

1. Sex involves highly charged, emotional stuff in which two egos can get all tied up in knots, making it a tough subject for anyone to discuss.

2. The Drive Like Me syndrome. People tend to think they are great drivers and believe if others would drive like they do, traffic problems would disappear. Similarly, the belief around sexual enjoyment might be: "I simply need to enlighten you to grasp the way, the truth, and the light, and you'll get turned on just like I do!" Not true, of course. Each person is unique in what turns him or her on.

3. This is a very private event, the most private of all human experiences. That quality makes us uncomfortable when bringing sexuality out into the daylight.

Despite these reasons, it's critical to be able to discuss the topic with your partner—especially if you're deliberately investing in a future of sexual happiness. No more lives of quiet desperation. Talk about it!

❦

Titillating Tips
Kat's communication techniques: "What to do if …"

No matter what you need to discuss with your partner, never do it in bed. When you feel relaxed, committed, and open, find a neutral place and time. Here are some tough questions that might come up:

What to say if …

- *You have to ask if your partner is "clean"*: "I just had my blood tests [make sure you've had them!]. I'm happy to announce that I am clean of STIs, and I have my results to share with you. How about you?" If they say no, or they don't know, you have a choice: you can insist on no sex, or you can have sex with a condom. Unprotected sex is not an option.

- *You have to ask a partner to wear a condom*: "This is awkward for me, but let's use a condom. Here I have one [always carry one!]. Let me help you put it on." Sometimes men will tell you that they lose sensation. However, the new condoms today are not your father's condoms; they're ultra thin so most men actually cannot tell the difference between condoms on or off. In any case, you must protect yourself. No one else will!

- *You have to tell your partner that you have an STI:* "Before we begin, I want you to wear a condom. I had a diagnosis of positive for genital herpes (for example). The condom will protect you from getting it during intercourse. Have you been checked?" If you have an STI, know your symptoms, when you are contagious, when not. Do not have sex when open sores are present. Know when sexual activity is appropriate for you.

- *You have to tell your partner you want to change the way you do certain things in bed:* "I love the way we make love. One thing I love that you do is _____ (say something positive). When we do this _____ (activity you want changed), I'd love for you to do more of this _____ and less of this _____ ." Be specific in your directions. Feel free to acknowledge if it feels awkward. And make sure you reinforce the actions you enjoy while you're doing them. Say, "This feels so good!"

If you want to make it short and sweet, use this three-part statement:

1. *"When you do this _____ ."* (State the activity, such as "when you give me oral sex.")

2. *"This is what happens _____ ."* (Explain what you want to have changed, such as "you use your teeth in a little nibble, and I don't think you realize it, but it hurts me.")

3. *"Next time I'd like you to do it this way _____ ."* (State what you would like to have happen next

time, such as "I'd like you to use your tongue more in that little flicking motion and not use your teeth at all.")

Talking about your intimate needs can be, at best, challenging and, at worst, terrifying. Even in solid, long-term relationships, it can be difficult to discuss feelings, attitudes, needs, and wants about sex. Try the following "Yours, Mine, Ours" exercise. It allows you the freedom to ask for what you want and need. Be sure to listen to the needs of your partner *without judgment.*

❧

Titillating Tip
Yours, Mine, and Ours …

Make a list of what you like sexually and have your partner do the same. Then compare the lists, circling what you both like on the lists. Place your items under Yours, Mine, and Ours. Then one night, you do what *you* want; another night, you do what *he* wants; a third night, you do an activity from the Ours list—something you know you'll both enjoy.

For example, if you like to have dinner at a restaurant as a sexual warm-up, you can do that on *your* night. If he likes to take showers with you, he gets to do that on *his* night. On the night that's designated Ours, both of you select something you'd enjoy together. This way, everyone gets his/her needs met. What a great win-win for both of you!

Now that you know what you want and how to ask for it, let's look at a dilemma that merits a lot of discussion: Body Image. In Part IV, you'll learn more about unleashing your seasoned sexuality into the realm of new possibilities.

Part Four

BODY IMAGE—
TALES OF AGE GAIN

When I was facilitating sex education for medical students at the University of Cincinnati Medical School, I had the privilege of hearing Dr. Paul Pearsall, one of the world's all-time pillars of sexuality education.

At the time, Dr. Pearsall was the director of the Kinsey Institute of Indiana University, the leader in sexuality research. He began his keynote to the young interns with this anecdote about body image and their future patients: "You need only remember two points: A woman's breasts come in two sizes—too big and too small. A man's penis comes in one size—too small." After the laughs subsided, he proclaimed, "Do no harm. Your sensitivity to your patients' insecurities will be the trust factor that builds relationships."

Dr. Pearsall was addressing body image—how we see ourselves. Body image has become muddied by a mishmash of our numerical age, our youth-worshipping culture, and airbrushed images from Madison Avenue-style advertising.

Both seasoned men and seasoned women have body image issues that can be huge. In fact, at the **Sex on the Porch** event, I always get a question that involves "how can I feel sexy with this aging body?" Just as weight gain challenges us, so does age gain. Let's see what we can do about it!

CHAPTER 9

Changes, Ugh!

"Most women want to be told they look at least ten years younger."
~ Kat

Let's be real. I want to look 25 again, don't you? Okay, I'll go for 35. Never mind, forget it. Let's do 45. Not that there's anything wrong with feeling good about looking 50 or 60 or 70. It's refreshing, encouraging, and wonderful to see healthy, robust 50, 60, 70+ers.

But honestly, out of the hundreds of women I've worked with, very few are happy with the way they look naturally—no matter what age they are. Most want to be told they look at least ten years younger. Very few (if any) women at midlife and beyond want anyone to describe them this way: "She looks healthy, robust, and beautiful (so far, so good) *and* she really looks her age (ouch)!"

❧

Highlights from Sex on the Porch

Pat, 64, said, "I feel old and ugly. I am embarrassed to be seen without clothes. I'm middle aged and I look middle aged. No one wants to see that in bed (including me). Help."

> Judy, also 64, said, "Feeling comfortable in my own skin? Now, more than ever, at our age, it's what it's about, I'm told. I get that part. So, how in the heck do I *do it?*"

I don't know about you, but I've been disliking parts of my body all my life. I remember as a teenager sunbathing at my Aunt Kay's pool near Detroit. Mind you, I was a competitive swimmer who worked out *strenuously* every day. Because my mother's mantra was "eat an apple," I didn't grow up on junk food. I was *not* fat.

But there I was, in my green two-piece bathing suit lying on a lawn chaise (the aluminum kind woven with the plastic ribbons in a plaid effect) when my five-year-old niece, Missy, came up to me and asked, "Kathy, is there a baby in your tummy?" At age 16, in that split second, I learned the meaning of "out of the mouths of babes." Horrified, I looked down to see what was showing up as a huge abnormal mound of flesh in my lower abdomen. After I told her I was *not* pregnant, I waited for the death blow—asking me what that bulge was from, if not a baby. Blessedly, she lost interest in my fat stomach and skipped away. But her unabashed honesty confirmed what I had feared most: *the whole world* noticed my protruding belly. How could I ever get a boyfriend sporting belly fat like that?

Today, as an adult, I can reframe her comment from a grown-up perspective. Nonetheless, I still carry the wound of overreaction from that vulnerable day. What helps are acknowledging these three observations:

1. My stomach is actually not all *that* big (although the gremlin still shouts at me, YES IT IS, KAT. Don't lie!). Women *have* tummies, for crying out loud. Look at Venus de Milo.

2. Missy was *only five* at the time of her verbal assault on me. My rational mind recognizes that her comment had nothing to do with the size of my tummy. Perhaps because her mother had recently given birth to her brother, she curiously thought all grown-up women were pregnant.

3. No man I have ever known at any time in my 62 years has ever cared or commented about the size of my belly. Still, I obsessively fight the obvious; they just never had the nerve to mention it.

Of course, these points seem to lend a blinding flash of the obvious to anyone who has ever suffered a body image insult. *There is nothing abnormal about the size of my tummy.* Nonetheless, if you have carried unnecessary sensitivity through the years, adopting rational realizations like these can be breakthroughs.

It's highly possible you've carried body issues with you, too, since childhood—or perhaps some have appeared with age. Naturally, yours are different than mine, but they might still cause you to obsess. For example, I'm small-breasted and big-tummied. As I swing up and down the weight scale, those two body parts seem to grow disproportionately—that is, the breasts tend to get smaller while the tummy gets bigger. I spend many moments in front of the mirror, standing at the right angle, of course, to see if anything has improved since the last time I checked (usually the night before). What disappointment; nothing has changed.

Nonetheless, there I stand, stomach sucked in, butt tucked under, shoulders back, pushing out those little breast beauties the best I can. (Why am I always dismayed at how far out they fail to go?) I throw in the towel, slouch, let my stomach stick out, and watch those tiny boobies sink flatly onto my chest. Then I heave a big sigh and reach a crossroads: Do I finish off the gelato or slap myself out of this pity party?

If you deem private mirror scrutiny difficult, nowhere is the challenge of feeling good about your body more evident than in the bedroom—the epicenter of body image drama.

The most sensitive parts come under the most intense scrutiny while involved in the most private of human activities: sex. Whether you're making deep, intimate love or having casual recreational sex, or even pleasuring yourself, the urge to self-denigrate the body bubbles up.

Bluntly stated, we women just don't like how we look. Having probed into the topic at **Sex on the Porch**, about a quarter of us could not find *one single thing* we liked about our bodies.

Exactly what do we worry about? Unacceptable breasts and general body malaise makes the top of the A list. The B list provides a host of other anxiety provokers: weight, tummy, thighs, facial features, skin (especially the fear of appearing like a deeply wrinkled Shar Pei dog when looking down at partner), upper arms, vulva shape, body hair. (No doubt you have your own order of discontent.)

With all this dissatisfaction going on, who can relax and enjoy sex?

Body Image in American Culture

Look around. In magazines, on TV, in movies, in shop windows, on the Internet, in travel brochures, on posters, even on street lamps, the female models you might try to emulate tend to have a body weight that is one-fifth to one-quarter less than the average American woman. That means if a normal woman tips the scales at

150 pounds, the model (who coyly suggests how you should look) weighs in at 117 pounds.

I don't know about you, but I continue to believe I'll put on that Saks outfit and look exactly like the model in the ad. I'm always disappointed.

How far will women go to alter their bodies from a natural state? According to the website of the American Society for Aesthetic Plastic Surgery (ASAPS), 10 million cosmetic procedures were performed in 2009 in the U.S. to the tune of $10.5 billion (that's *billion* with a B).

To give you some perspective, 10 million equates to every resident of New York City (including all five boroughs, not just Manhattan) having plastic surgery *plus every NYC tourist who visited that year!* And of those 10 million procedures, women underwent more than 90% of them. Almost 44 percent ($4.5 million) were for women ages 35-50, 27% for ages 51-64, and 7% for ages 65 and above.

As the ASAPS study indicated, the top procedures (in order of frequency) were:

- Breast augmentation (boob job)
- Liposuction (suction-assisted fat removal)
- Eyelid surgery (raise sagging eyelids)
- Rhinoplasty (nose job)
- Abdominoplasty (tummy tuck)

I am not judging here. Plastic surgery can change people's lives for the better if their brains and their hearts are convinced it's the best answer. In fact, all those things women do to please—clothes, make-up, cleavage, spike heels, sexy lingerie, plastic surgery—

come down to asking one important question: *Are you doing it for someone else or to please yourself?* If it's to please another person, find out why.

I'm serious about this. Check your motive. In my opinion, the only reason to enhance your body image is so you feel better *for yourself,* not anyone else.

My seasoned male clients tell me they're not exactly thrilled with their god-given attributes either. The A list for men is short: the penis. Then the B list: abs, pecs, body hair (too much on the corpus, not enough on the head), weight, height.

Our culture reflects this penile preference. Some male mannequins are sporting substantial bulges in their pants and chests unattainable even with steroids—not to mention that the pornography industry auditions for penis length. (Hey, guys! Women are much less concerned about the size of your penis than you are. Women, help me out here. I believe we're willing and able to adapt to his "length" if we find his *personality* attractive. Guys, that means your penis size, your weight, your pecs, and your abs are just fine as they are.)

Do men care about all the accoutrements women don? Men say an occasional "yes" to the obvious teasers—high heels, low-cut tank tops, and sexy underwear. Mostly, they say, "No, a woman's attitude wins out over her appearance." Healthy men will say what appeals is admiring the female body in whatever form it takes.

Remember this: Body perfection is not in the equation when men make love to a partner they truly care about.

❦

Kat's Quip
Wear What You Love

If you *feel sexy*, you *act sexy.* And when you feel uncomfortable being all dressed up, you act uncomfortable. Go ahead and enjoy all the physical enhancements you want—clothes, jewelry, and plastic surgery—but only if it pleases *you* in the doing and wearing. Never, never get plastic surgery for someone else. Wear outfits that you love, and if your partner admires them, too, that's a welcome bonus.

Do it for yourself, first. Own it!

CHAPTER 10

Own It!
You are What You Think You Are

Do any of the worries about your body affect your ability to:

- enjoy sex?

- enjoy relationships?

- meet people?

- even get out of bed in the morning?

If your answer to any of these is "yes," consider this: What you look like has nothing to do with your success in bed. Why? Because your brain is the biggest sex organ of all. *You have the power to program it for success or failure.* It's that simple.

The good news? Your brain will follow your instructions. The bad news? Same. Let's start with men. If your boyfriend says to himself, "My penis is too small. She will hate it." Guess what? It is and she will. On the other hand, if his self-directives sound like this: "I love satisfying my woman with my penis. She will love it." Guess what? He does and she will, too.

Flip the scenario to you. If you say to yourself, "My breasts sag too much. He will hate them." Guess what? Conversely, if you say, "My breasts are my pride and joy. I love the sensitivity and being touched there," you will project eroticism around your breasts. That's the attitude that gets picked up by your partner. Presto! You feel better. And he loves your breasts because you love them.

Titillating Tips
Handling jealousy when your man looks at another woman

Many of the women at **Sex on the Porch** complain about their partners looking at other women's breasts. Some even get angry and berate them for doing it. Women, stop the presses! Men are hard-wired to look and look and look. Their looking has *nothing* to do with you, your weight, your sagging breasts, your tiny breasts, your larger-than-life breasts, or your age.

My advice is this: Appreciate what he's doing as a healthy look and let the jealousy go. He's simply participating in the life-giving energy of sexuality. And know that, when he appreciates other women's breasts, he's enjoying yours as well. When he admires other breasts but has made a commitment to you, you *both* can admire the other breasts. You can even bring that energy back into your erotic adventures while appreciating the wonders of human sexuality.

In fact, I have checked out this advice with a plethora of men who all agree; they're in awe of the female body. *That's* what they admire. It's not a slam on you; in truth, it's a compliment to you.

If women can grasp this concept, everyone is happier. Men don't feel punished for their natural hard wiring, and women appreciate the life force of sexuality everyone experiences. Wise couples bring that energy into the bedroom.

Facing Fitting Room Fear

No doubt you've had to do this, too: shop for clothes in an environment where you have to take off your clothes in front of another person such as a friend or sales associate. Not a problem at 25 years old, but it's a problem for most women over 50. Ice runs through your veins. There you stand in front of the mirror in your skivvies, just your body and the looking glass. You think, "Who *is* that woman in the mirror? Seriously, that isn't my body! I don't *really* look like that, do I?" Does this sound familiar?

For me, my arms look like my grandmother's dimpled sagging skin. Cringe. It's true. I remember thinking how *comfortable* her arms looked—as a child. Now? On me? No way. Turns out that truly believing the adage "know that your inner beauty is shining through" is harder than you might think, especially when you're shopping for clothes. It takes serious focus.

In that fitting room, the body revulsion leads to strong thoughts like this: "This is *me* who, prior to my age gain, was the epitome of body tightness. My body was the temple of my soul. Riding my bike, eating a good diet, lifting weights, walking all over at turbo speed. Fitness was my middle name. Yet, there I am, dimpled, humiliated, and flabby with the best of them." Mind chatter like this can sink your self-esteem faster than the Titanic. It's critical to stop these thoughts before they take over. At midlife-plus, more than ever, treating ourselves to new drapery for our beautiful bodies is essential. Your body is *still* the temple of your soul; as such, it deserves to be well adorned. That principle doesn't change with age.

Thank your amazing body and delight yourself by ornamenting it with lovely accoutrements. It's all about your 'tude.

༄

Titillating Tips
"Do I look beautiful in this?"

The next time you're alone in a fitting room with a stack of clothes that looked fabulous on the manikin, do this:

1. Get your head screwed on right *before* you enter the dressing room. Be real. You're not 25. Accept that your body is doing pretty darn well considering the stress you have put it through for all those years. Be gentle with yourself.

2. Immediately stop the nasty self-hate thoughts when they start.

3. Don't ask anyone if an outfit makes you look fat. If you have to ask, it doesn't matter what the answer is. You'll never wear it.

4. Only ask, *"Do I feel beautiful in this?"* not *"Do I look good?"* Big difference. Whether you're buying bras, earrings, or a suit for the office, your answer should always be YES. Any other answer means DON'T BUY IT.

CHAPTER 11

It's All About Your 'Tude, Not Your Age Gain

Understanding your unique strengths and your insecurities will help you highlight your best while overcoming your feelings of doubt. Let's pinpoint where you feel great about yourself so you can accentuate the positive parts and downplay the insecure areas.

How you respond to the following statements will help you see how your body image affects your sexuality and give you clues about your dress for personal focus. Answering "True" to all of the following means you soar in confidence. However, if you answer "False" to many of these statements, no worries. I have not met a single woman who answers "True" to all of these!

As you write down your answers, be truthful but also be easy on yourself. There are no right answers, just heightened awareness.

T or F	Question
	I have a favorite body part and I can easily name it.
	When I look in the mirror naked, I see an attractive body.
	I know exactly which styles of clothes compliment my body, and I'm assertive about seeking these styles.
	I never make apologies for my body (weight gain, weight loss, illness, injury, etc.) when I'm in a fitting room with another person.

T or F	Question
	I always simply say "thank you" when someone compliments me.
	I don't compare myself to other women.
	I feel comfortable wearing a bathing suit when on vacation.
	When a partner looks at my naked body, I feel comfortable.
	When a partner looks at my genitals, I feel comfortable.
	I never hide certain body parts during sex.
	Having lights on during romantic interludes is okay with me.
	I would never end a relationship because of the way my body looks.
	If I had plastic surgery, it would be because I wanted it, not for anyone else.

Your Body Image Sensitivity

Look at the specific body parts listed in the following chart, check what's true for you, and make helpful comments. Take time to really notice how you feel about each one. This will help you get an overall picture of your body image sensitivity.

Body part	I like it	I don't like it	I accept this body part unconditionally (with comments)
Body in general			
Face in general			
Hair			
Cheeks			
Eyes			

Body part	I like it	I don't like it	I accept this body part unconditionally (with comments)
Nose			
Lips			
Ears/Earlobes			
Neck			
Shoulders			
Breasts - shape			
Breasts - size			
Belly			
Back			
Buttocks			
Arms			
Elbows			
Hands			
Fingers			
Thighs			
Calves			
Knees			
Ankles			
Feet in general			
Toes			
Genitals - clitoris			
Genitals - vulva area			
Genitals - pubic hair			
Anus			

Remember this above all: Women's bodies are meant to be enjoyed! If you need help doing so, there is no shame in working with a professional to heal body image issues so you can be the sexy, desirable person you were meant to be. The glorious body you have needs to be celebrated! Own it!

～⁓

Titillating Tips
For seasoned confidence …

Follow these basic tenets for living happily and lovingly in your sexy seasoned body:

1. Look at your relatives and know that you inherited 70 percent of what you've been dealt. Learn which aspects you can change and which ones you can't. Live with the conclusions.

2. Say thank you to your body for all the hard work it has done to bring you this far. It's not easy living with all the stress and exhaustion you have put it through over 55, 65, 75 years!

3. If you make physical improvements including plastic surgery, do it *only* because *you* will feel better doing so, not anyone else.

4. Remember that the ideal does not exist. All those actors and fashion models—even the older ones—have been professionally made up and their photos airbrushed. At the end of the day, their make-up comes off, and they go home, make dinner, and pay bills just like the rest of us.

5. Your male counterparts face body image issues, too. Be gentle with them, as you would want them to be with you.

6. Take pressure off yourself and others to be perfect. Relax. Know that the confidence and assertiveness that ripens with age is sexier than what any prancing 25 year old offers. Yes, in the short term, that cute 20-something body will turn heads. In the long run, however, it's the attitude and self-assurance that only comes with age that wins. Confidence, not performance, gets the attention.

7. Take these actions:

   • Stop looking at fitness and fashion magazines.

   • Start communicating with your partner about how you feel.

   • Learn to manage your emotions well.

   • Develop a spiritual connection.

   • Get professional help if your body image prevents you from feeling confidence and pleasure.

8. Strut your stuff. You are a beautiful seasoned woman! Walk away from that counter with a little swing in your hip. Let them look at you! Get rid of your turtlenecks; show a bit of cleavage; buy yourself a new pair of earrings the first of every month. When you make eye contact, smile wisely and nod. Throw your shoulders back and show off those beauties. Let the seasoned confidence burst forth!

Change your attitude and you change the outcome. Easy? Not always, given the age gain you're experiencing. Tell your brain and body that "you are beautiful" and you will be!

Bottom line: It's all in how you perceive your world and the attitude you project. Age gain can be wonderful. Enjoy your seasoned female body (and the "sexperiences" it provides) just the way it is—erotically intact and ready to be adored and adorned. Own it!

Go forth and try out all the new possibilities …

I Propose a Toast

Dear Sexy Seasoned Woman,

This is my desire for you: To revive passion, re-energize your sexuality, re-invigorate your sexy self, and for years to come, be the unique, vibrant, sensual woman you are—however *you* define it.

I hope you have accepted my invitation to participate fully in the festivities of intimacy and sexuality in whatever way works best for you. Always remember, being sexy is supposed to be fun!

I also hope you have had a blast with *Sexperienced.* Hand this book around to all your friends. Yes, you all *deserve* to have a grand time enjoying yourself in the bedroom, on the boulevard, and as a seasoned woman.

Here's a toast to many years of seasoned sexuality filled with a myriad of possibilities for you, the beautiful, sexy woman you are! Stand tall and Own It!

Warmly,

Kat Forsythe

ABOUT *the* AUTHOR

Katherine Anne Forsythe, MSW ("Kat") is well known for her passionate belief that vitality as a woman and sexual happiness are our birthright; they're part of our wholeness as men and women throughout our lives.

Kat is an expert in the continuum of sexual intimacy and relationships for the Baby Boomer plus crowd. Her mantra, "Own it!" rings joyfully in the heads and hearts of clients, workshop participants, and those who know her through her media and online presence.

Kat provides seminars for singles and couples, webinars to invigorate seasoned sexuality, and private sessions for both couples and singles who seek discreet help in dating, intimacy, and issues of sexuality. Kat's monthly event, **Sex on the Porch**, empowers women at midlife-plus to get their "sexy" back—in the bedroom and on the boulevard.

Please visit www.getasecondwind.com to:

- Discover helpful tips to enhance your relationship.
- Read about practical solutions to support you during your intimate challenges.
- Register for a **Sex on the Porch** event.
- Sign up for Kat's *Get A Second Wind* newsletter.
- Reserve a spot at a weekend event for singles or couples.
- Order products mentioned in *Sexperienced.*
- Arrange a discreet private counseling session with Kat.

Kat holds an MSW from the University of Cincinnati with an emphasis on human sexuality and aging. Her postgraduate studies include The National Sexuality Resource Center at San Francisco State. She is a member of the Consortium on Sex and Aging at Widener University, American Association of Sex Educators, Counselors, and Therapists, and the Society for the Scientific Study of Sexuality.

ACKNOWLEDGMENTS

To all of you who pushed, pulled, encouraged, mandated, suggested, threatened, and cajoled me into the creation of this book, Thank You! You know who you are. I couldn't have done this without you—a labor of love!

Special thanks to these mentors and cheerleaders who stood by me steadfastly throughout the process, offering an endless stream of wisdom and encouragement:

- Dr. Patti Britton
- Debbie Josendale
- Ann Tardy
- Margaret Sutherland, PhD
- Joseph Hanson, Jr.
- Gail Webber
- Linda Wildey
- Heidi Green
- Jean Schore

Thank You!

www.ingramcontent.com/pod-product-compliance
Lightning Source LLC
LaVergne TN
LVHW061224060426
835509LV00012B/1412